MODERN ETIQUETTE
WEDDING PLANNER

Modern Etiquette Wedding Planner

The Essential Organizer to
Make Your Day Special for Everyone

ELISABETH KRAMER

ROCKRIDGE
PRESS

Interior and Cover Designer: Michael Cook
Art Producer: Janice Ackerman
Editor: John Makowski
Production Editor: Mia Moran and Ruth Sakata Corley
Production Manager: Martin Worthington

Illustration: ©lavendertime/istock
Author Photo: Courtesy of Marissa Solini Photography

Paperback ISBN: 978-1-63807-410-6
eBook ISBN: 978-1-63807-241-6

R0

FOR G.,
WHO TAUGHT ME SO MUCH
ABOUT LOVE.

CONTENTS

INTRODUCTION

Congratulations on your engagement! Or should I say, "Welcome to your new part-time job!" On average, it takes nearly 10 hours a week to plan a wedding. With an engagement lasting an average of 14 months, that's 560 hours spent planning *before* the actual wedding day.

If your stomach dropped while reading that last paragraph, never fear. You're in the right place. The goal of this book is to make sure that all of your time, effort, and money pays off.

First, though, a little backstory: I am a professional wedding planner who, as of this writing, has helped plan more than 50 weddings, including my own. What I've learned is that there's no such thing as the perfect wedding. Believing that there is quickly turns one of life's most joyful rituals into a burden that couples loathe and regret.

I used to think that this nasty reality was the couple's fault. I've since learned that it's not. Much of the pressure a couple feels while wedding planning comes from what's called the "wedding industrial complex."

For me, that term refers to all of the nasty -isms we encounter throughout our lives, including but not limited to racism, ageism, ableism, and homophobia (which I realize is not an -ism, but you get the idea). That same hate is present in the wedding industry, except it's wrapped up in tulle and used to make you feel like you need to look a certain way or spend a certain amount of money or do a certain thing to achieve perfection.

I think this is gross and so have devoted my career to fighting the wedding industrial complex. This book is part of that fight because, when used with intention, etiquette can be an extremely effective tool in making the wedding industry—and thus, your wedding—better.

As such, I invite you to reconsider what we mean when we use the word "etiquette." When I use it, I don't mean "Which fork goes where?" I mean *empathy*. How we treat others and ourselves is key to accomplishing our mission of creating a celebration that is as expansive, awe-inspiring, and miraculous as love.

Often, we call that celebration a "wedding," and when it's done with intention, I believe a wedding can transcend a typical party. It can create the best feeling in the entire universe: pure joy.

Last thing and then we'll get to the good stuff: The advice in this book is inherently flawed because it comes from me, an inherently flawed human being. I'm also limited by my lived experience as a cisgender, heterosexual, white woman who is not living with a disability.

I have done my best to offer advice that does not actively harm other humans. Anything that doesn't serve you and your love, please ignore. This includes if your love is not a two-partner relationship. However you honor love, I hope this book helps.

And with that, please grab your favorite writing implement, beverage of choice, and chosen life partner(s). Let's work together to plan a wedding worthy of your love.

A QUICK NOTE ON LANGUAGE

Wedding. I use the word "wedding" to refer to any celebration that recognizes the start of a marriage. This includes elopements, micro-weddings, and mini-monies. To me, they're all the same thing: weddings.

VIP. I opt for the term "VIP" throughout most of this book. The term refers to anyone whom you want to have more information than your average guest. You may recognize these more common but gendered and not universally applicable words: maid or matron of honor, bridesmaid, best man, groomsman, mother of the bride, father of the bride, mother of the groom, father of the groom, flower girl, and ring bearer. My use of VIP also includes people like ceremony readers who are doing a certain job that other guests aren't.

Vendor. Most often, the word "vendor" refers to anyone being paid to perform a certain function at your wedding. However, depending on what that person is doing, vendor can also refer to someone who performs a certain function but is not being paid, such as your friend who is also a DJ.

Etiquette. When I use the word "etiquette," I mean the Golden Rule: How do we treat others and ourselves to create a celebration that prioritizes safety and joy?

1

Wedding Vision

If you and your partner have been engaged for more than five seconds, someone has probably asked about your vision. Usually, the question comes from a well-meaning loved one or eager-to-please wedding vendor who may or may not be clutching your left hand and ogling your engagement ring.

I am a professional wedding planner, and I have never taken to the word "vision" when used in relation to wedding planning. To me, a vision is something you see while lost in the desert. It's a mirage, and running toward it can do more harm than good.

That doesn't mean I think we should entirely discount the question; we just need to reframe it. When we say, "What is your vision?" what we actually mean is, "What is your goal?" And more specifically, "What is the goal of your wedding?" Thankfully, we already know the answer: to start your marriage.

Etiquette helps because if we focus on what serves your marriage rather than what serves your wedding, we'll accomplish both goals. By keeping your marriage in mind, we'll plan a wedding that's in line with your values as a couple because we are thinking so actively about what your values are for your marriage. The result is an event custom-tailored to celebrate what you and your partner hold dear.

So I'll ask you again: What is your vision—not for your wedding but for your marriage?

Here and throughout the book, we'll look at how some couples have approached wedding planning, with positive and negative results for themselves and their guests.

COUPLE 1

Andrew and Tre were so overwhelmed by the expectations of their family that they began to fight frequently while planning their wedding. As a result, they were exhausted by the time their wedding arrived. What would have helped? Remembering the most important question in all of wedding planning: Why do we want to have a wedding?

COUPLE 2

Katrina and Jocelyn invited 113 guests to their wedding, but one of the most important people couldn't attend. Katrina's dad died when she was a teen. Many of the guests knew her father, and it was important to Katrina that he be recognized. She did this in several ways, including wearing a necklace her dad made and walking down the aisle with her mom as a beloved family song played. The recognition gave the guests and the couple space to honor the past and celebrate the future.

TOP FIVE ETIQUETTE DOS

1. **Do take a moment to breathe.** It's very easy to hop on the wedding planning merry-go-round. Instead, savor your engagement. Take a day or a week or a month. Usually, there is no rush to get married. But if there is, you can still take an afternoon to enjoy yourself.

2. **Do set a regular check-in.** Rather than cram in wedding planning on your lunch hour, consider setting a regular check-in as a couple. Weekly, bimonthly, or monthly all work well.

3. **Do expect to repeat yourself.** You'll quickly realize that people ask the same exact questions after learning you're engaged. Keep your patience by remembering that they're asking these seemingly inane questions because they want to connect with you over a very special event, but they don't always know what to say.

4. **Do celebrate.** After the initial hugs, kisses, and calls, we often default to scrolling on our phones as we begin wedding planning. Avoid this. Instead, take your partner out on a date. Use that time to start brainstorming. Have fun. Collaborate.

5. **Do remember that two people are getting married, not just one.** You are about to begin what may be the most sexist experience of your life. You may field bigoted questions and ghosting from vendors. You may also be surprised at how quickly wedding planning is expected to become one partner's responsibility over another's. None of this is your fault, and you'll weather the storm better if you face it together.

TOP FIVE ETIQUETTE DON'TS

1. **Don't hesitate to say, "We don't know yet."** As soon as people learn you're planning a wedding, they'll want to know when, where, and if they're invited. These questions can really get under your skin. A simple "We don't know yet" is a perfectly polite answer. It's also a satisfactory one for the person who asked. They were only trying to celebrate this moment with you, not expecting a fully developed plan.

2. **Don't post before you call.** If you can, tell your most immediate loved ones that you and your partner are engaged before you make a broader announcement.

3. **Don't feel compelled to tell the world.** Don't feel bad if you want to share your news online, but also don't feel like you have to. Your engagement can be just as special without a hashtag.

4. **Don't assume anything.** I often hear the words "I had no idea that [insert loved one's name] cared so much about . . ." Weddings bring out all kinds of things in people, so don't assume that someone you love will act a certain way. You wouldn't want them to expect this of you, so don't expect it of them.

5. **Don't minimize how your engagement makes you feel.** I was surprised at how different I felt after I got engaged. I thought it meant I wasn't a "good" feminist. Don't do this to yourself. Getting engaged is the beginning of a huge transition in a couple's relationship, no matter who they are or what they believe. Give yourself grace.

SHARED VALUES WORKSHEET

Answer these questions together as a couple.

What are three words that we would use to describe our relationship to a complete stranger?

What are the three (G-rated) activities that we most strongly associate doing together?

If we had a family motto, what would it be? Why?

CONSIDER THIS

It can be useful to have a sense of the industry that you two are about to participate in so you can keep your wits about you and hold true to your values as a couple.

- The average length of an engagement in the United States is 13.6 months.
- The average cost of a wedding in the United States is $28,000.
- On average, it takes 10 hours a week to plan a wedding.
- The US wedding industry makes an annual average of $72 billion.

WEDDING VISION WORKSHEET

Make a duplicate of this worksheet (on your phone, computer, or a separate piece of paper) so you and your partner both have a copy.

Part 1

Fill this out separately and privately. Ideally, you'll do this at the same time.

What's the one thing that I hate most about other people's weddings?

_____

_____

_____

What's the one thing that I love most about other people's weddings?

_____

_____

_____

How do I want to feel on my wedding day? (Try to use just one word.)

_____

Why do I want to have a wedding?

_____

_____

_____

_____

_____

Part 2

Share your answers to Part 1 with each other. Then answer the following together.

What was similar about our answers?

_____

_____

_____

_____

_____

What was different about our answers?

_____

_____

_____

What surprised us in each other's answers?

Part 3

Use Part 1 and Part 2 to develop a one-sentence wedding mission statement.
Examples:

1. The mission of our wedding is to treat a select group of family members to a high-quality meal.

2. Our mission is to have the most outrageous dance party of our lives.

3. We want to experience a once-in-a-lifetime trip with our friends.

DESTINATION WEDDING

The term "destination wedding" usually evokes palm trees. But whether you're getting married at the beach two hours from your home or flying to a whole other country, most weddings are a destination for someone on your guest list.

The trick is to remember that whatever choice you make probably won't work for everyone you care about. That's okay. Consider who must physically be at your wedding for it to feel like your wedding, and prioritize the needs of those people after your own as a couple.

When it comes to destination, please also prioritize safety. You want to make sure that your destination is inclusive and welcoming to all, no matter their race, religion, gender, or sexual orientation. For LGBTQIA+ couples, this means picking a spot that is both safe for your love and, potentially, where you can legally begin your marriage. Consulting the US State Department's recommendations for LGBTQIA+ travelers is a good place to start.

OUR WEDDING PRIORITIES

Fill out this worksheet together. Where you disagree, talk through why a certain element does or does not have personal value to you. Work toward compromise.

Part 1

Here is a list of the most common wedding vendors. Rank these on a scale of 1 to 15, with 1 as the most important for accomplishing your wedding mission statement and 15 the least important.

_____ Caterer (*appetizer, bar, breakfast/lunch/dinner, dessert*)

_____ Flowers and/or florist

_____ Hair and/or makeup

_____ Jeweler

.... Music (*DJ, live band, etc.*)

.... Officiant(s) (*i.e., who is legally marrying you*)

.... Photographer

.... Photo booth

.... Planner

.... Printmaker (*think: letterpress invites*)

.... Rentals (*this will likely only be highly ranked if you're trying to create a certain space and/or your venue(s)/caterer(s) won't provide these items already*)

.... Transportation

.... Venue(s)

.... Videographer

.... What you're wearing to the wedding

From the list in Part 1:

What are our top five vendors? This is what we should plan to spend the most money on.

_____

_____

_____

_____

_____

What are our middle five vendors? This is what we should plan to spend less money on.

_____

_____

_____

_____

_____

What are our bottom five vendors? This is what we should spend the least money on or skip entirely.

_____

_____

_____

_____

_____

Part 2

Below is a list of wedding "traditions." Pretend you can only do one at your wedding. Which would you each pick and why? Circle and discuss. (Only consider those that are applicable to you and your partner.)

- Exchanging rings
- Giving away of one partner to another
- Lifting of the veil
- Reception introduction
- Toasts
- First dances (examples: couple, VIP/Partner 1, VIP/Partner 2)
- Cake-cutting and/or first bite
- Bouquet and/or garter toss
- Send-off

CONTENTS

INTRODUCTION

Congratulations on your engagement! Or should I say, "Welcome to your new part-time job!" On average, it takes nearly 10 hours a week to plan a wedding. With an engagement lasting an average of 14 months, that's 560 hours spent planning *before* the actual wedding day.

If your stomach dropped while reading that last paragraph, never fear. You're in the right place. The goal of this book is to make sure that all of your time, effort, and money pays off.

First, though, a little backstory: I am a professional wedding planner who, as of this writing, has helped plan more than 50 weddings, including my own. What I've learned is that there's no such thing as the perfect wedding. Believing that there is quickly turns one of life's most joyful rituals into a burden that couples loathe and regret.

I used to think that this nasty reality was the couple's fault. I've since learned that it's not. Much of the pressure a couple feels while wedding planning comes from what's called the "wedding industrial complex."

For me, that term refers to all of the nasty -isms we encounter throughout our lives, including but not limited to racism, ageism, ableism, and homophobia (which I realize is not an -ism, but you get the idea). That same hate is present in the wedding industry, except it's wrapped up in tulle and used to make you feel like you need to look a certain way or spend a certain amount of money or do a certain thing to achieve perfection.

I think this is gross and so have devoted my career to fighting the wedding industrial complex. This book is part of that fight because, when used with intention, etiquette can be an extremely effective tool in making the wedding industry—and thus, your wedding—better.

As such, I invite you to reconsider what we mean when we use the word "etiquette." When I use it, I don't mean "Which fork goes where?" I mean *empathy*. How we treat others and ourselves is key to accomplishing our mission of creating a celebration that is as expansive, awe-inspiring, and miraculous as love.

Often, we call that celebration a "wedding," and when it's done with intention, I believe a wedding can transcend a typical party. It can create the best feeling in the entire universe: pure joy.

WEDDING PLANNING IN A VIRTUAL WORLD

Wedding planning in the 21st century is both a blessing and a curse. Never before has it been so easy to quickly research your options. Never before has it been so easy to be completely and utterly overwhelmed by those same options.

Online resources are only as useful as you make them. If constantly scrolling Pinterest makes you break out in a cold sweat, stop. Options are just that: options. Use them to inform decisions that you and your partner have already made about elements you want to include, not to establish what you think you should have.

Also feel under no obligation to include a virtual option for your in-person wedding. Such options—such as livestreaming the ceremony or FaceTiming the toasts—grew popular during the COVID-19 pandemic. In many ways, this is good news. Zoom, Google Meet, and more wedding-specific streaming options offer a whole new set of tools to help people you love participate in your wedding day without necessarily having to travel or pay to attend.

But if you and your partner don't feel the mission statement of your wedding will be served by a virtual option, don't include it. Politely explain why. You can use language like "We have decided to not include a virtual element to our wedding but welcome texts, phone calls, and cards." Then move on.

THE PERFECT WEDDING

There's a nasty myth in wedding planning that if you plan the perfect wedding, you'll have a perfect marriage. That's fundamentally not true. Instead, think of your wedding as what it is: the birthday of your marriage.

Put your heads together and describe **your dream marriage.** What words do you want to describe it? What experiences do you want to have together? How do you each want your marriage to make you feel?

....

....

....

Now turn back to **your wedding.** How can this celebration usher in the values you have identified as important to your marriage? How can your wedding reflect your family motto? What is the mission statement of your wedding?

CONSIDER THIS

For many people, the legal ability to get married is a new and fragile right that is still not universally accessible. You do not need to stop everything to honor this, but please remember that having this choice is special, even during those times when planning your wedding feels tedious.

ONE-YEAR TIMELINE

12 MONTHS OUT
- Celebrate. You just got engaged!

11 MONTHS OUT
- Set a budget. *Be honest about what you can and can't afford. Discuss who's contributing what.*
- Decide where and when. *You and your partner can decide this without putting down a deposit.*
- Draft a guest list. *You don't need to tell anyone anything yet.*

10 MONTHS OUT

▶ Begin hiring. *Aim to research, interview, and officially hire one vendor a month.*

▶ Consider what you're wearing. *There's a good chance that whatever you're wearing will need time to be altered or made.*

9 MONTHS OUT

▶ Discuss what you want to communicate to guests. *This is the time to build a wedding website, arrange a hotel block, register for gifts, and/or take engagement photos.*

8 MONTHS OUT

▶ Consider who will be your VIPs.

▶ Start telling people. *While not required, couples often send two forms of guest communication: a save-the-date and an invite. If you're sending save-the-dates, send them in the next month or so. If you're skipping save-the-dates, consider sending invites between now and six months out from the wedding.*

7 MONTHS OUT

▶ Brainstorm your honeymoon. *If you're traveling internationally, don't forget to get or renew your passports, as needed.*

6 MONTHS OUT

▶ Vendor and VIPs checkpoint. *Where are we with hiring? Do our VIPs know the when and the where of our wedding?*

▶ Gut check. *How is each of us feeling?*

▶ Relationship checkup. *What's working now that we would like to keep working in our marriage? Consider premarital counseling.*

5 MONTHS OUT

▶ Do you want to party? *Examples include a wedding or bridal shower, a bachelor or bachelorette party, a rehearsal dinner, and a post-wedding brunch. Start brainstorming—and don't be afraid to ask for help.*

▶ Consider additional gifts. *If exchanging gifts is of value to you and your partner, consider what you might want to get your VIPs.*

4 MONTHS OUT

▶ Want wedding rings? *If so, begin researching your options.*

▶ Need insurance? *If your venue(s) require insurance, get what you need and send it over so you don't have to worry about it later.*

3 MONTHS OUT

▸ If you sent save-the-dates, now's the time to send invites. *And if you didn't send save-the-dates, you probably already sent invites. If not, do so now.*

▸ Book a trial. *Certain services such as hair and makeup may offer a trial. If applicable, you'll book this soon.*

▸ Consider decorations. *If you're making your own, develop a plan for what you need and when you're doing the work. Remember to consider any kind of seating chart, programs, menus, and/or favors that you may be giving out.*

2 MONTHS OUT

▸ Apply for your marriage license. *The specific window of time will vary depending on where you're getting married. Also keep an eye on any "waiting period" (i.e., the number of days you need to physically have the license before the wedding for the license to be legal).*

▸ Start your vows. *If you're writing your own, schedule a few sessions.*

▸ Consider a final walk-through. *This is a meeting at your venue(s) with you, your partner, a venue manager, and a planner and/or caterer (if applicable). Use it as a meeting of the minds to talk through timing, setup, and cleanup.*

1 MONTH OUT

▸ Make your wedding day timeline and vendor and VIP directory. *Aim to have both done no later than two weeks before your wedding. Then send customized versions of the timeline to every vendor and VIP. Include any vendor-specific details, such as song choices for a DJ or final guest count for a caterer or florist.*

▸ Start paying people. *Many of your payments are likely due this month.*

▸ Make sure your clothes are in order. *This includes shoes, undergarments, and accessories.*

▸ Plan a date night. *Carve out time for just you two before the whirlwind begins.*

2

Budget

The wedding industry perpetuates a very particular lie: If you spend more money, you'll have a better wedding, and if you have a better wedding, you'll have a better marriage. This is why couples often find themselves blowing their budgets on items they couldn't have cared less about before they got engaged.

In this chapter, we'll face the lie about money and wedding planning head-on. It won't be easy. As we discuss budget, you may find—if you haven't already—that everything costs a lot more than expected. You may wonder what the correct etiquette is when it comes to asking for money. You may even begin to doubt yourself when it comes to the value of certain goods. Are those Mason jars actually worth $45, or have you just lost your hold on reality?

Whatever happens, please remember one thing: Do not give in to the lie. You and your partner are trying to decide how much money to spend and where that money is coming from. You are not deciding the fate of your entire relationship. For better or worse, there is no set amount of money that you can spend on your wedding that will guarantee the success of your marriage. If there were, rich people would never get divorced.

COUPLE 1

Trisha and Jenn regularly forgot to pay their vendor team on time. The result was hurt feelings and worse service that led to an awkward, uncomfortable environment for all involved.

COUPLE 2

Khyrista and Robert hosted their wedding at a private resort; their ceremony site was at the base of a steep gravel incline. To accommodate the needs of their guests with limited mobility, they paid an extra $85 for a private golf cart to shuttle these guests up and down the hill.

TOP FIVE ETIQUETTE DOS

1. **Do expect the "wedding tax."** Like its evil twin the "pink tax," the wedding tax refers to a surcharge added to services for the sole reason that the service in question is happening for a wedding. There are some ways to work around it—the easiest being to just not say the word "wedding"—but that's not always possible. As such, add a 2 to 5 percent buffer to your big-ticket items. That should help until we root out the social attitudes that led to this tax.

2. **Do tip.** I know, I know. You've already spent so much on your wedding. But wedding vendors are service workers; tips make a difference.

3. **Do anticipate "hidden fees" and last-minute purchases.** That emergency run to the grocery store the night before is going to happen, so add an emergency fund to your wedding budget. It doesn't have to be much. And if you don't spend it, you'll have more money for life after the wedding!

4. **Do remember that everything has a cost.** It just depends on what you're spending: your money or your time. While many functions can be done on your own, don't fool yourself into thinking that DIY is the same as free. It's not.

5. **Do spend more money on the things you really want.** As in many elements of life, you often get what you pay for when it comes to wedding vendors. That's why the prioritization exercise later in this chapter is so important: It'll help you and your partner identify what you actually care about so you can pay a higher fee for a higher-quality product.

TOP FIVE ETIQUETTE DON'TS

1. **Don't immediately book a venue.** This is the number one mistake couples make when it comes to budget. They may feel such urgency to figure out when they're hosting a wedding that they immediately book a venue—only to realize the deposit was more than their whole budget.

2. **Don't buy things you don't actually want.** It's okay if this happens, but when you start to feel stressed, remember the list you'll make later in this chapter. What were these bottom three items? Why didn't we want them? Oh, that's right: because we wanted those top three items more.

3. **Don't be afraid to ask vendors why they charge what they charge.** Couples often assume that this is rude, but quality vendors have quality answers.

4. **Don't forget The Board.** Consider anyone who contributes money to your wedding a member of The Board. You don't have to run every decision by them, but do expect to hear them out when it's something they're paying for.

5. **Don't beat yourselves up.** No matter how you cut it, your wedding will be one of the most expensive things you ever pay for. Keep communicating with your partner. You'll feel worse if you don't.

HOW MUCH SHOULD WE SPEND?

Instead of starting with "should," ask this question: "How much do we *need* to spend on our wedding?" Then: "How much do we *want* to spend on our wedding?" And finally: "How much *should* we spend on our wedding?"

Each of those numbers will be different. That's exactly what we want. Use these three answers to arrive at the number we're actually looking for: "How much will we *actually* spend on our wedding?"

That final number will probably be different than you ever imagined, but that's okay because you haven't spent it yet. It's a measuring stick that you and your partner can gut-check certain purchases against. You can use it to ask yourselves: "Is this something that we're buying because we *need* to buy it, we *want* to buy it, or we *should* buy it? How much closer or further away does this purchase take us from the mission statement of our wedding?"

WAYS TO SAVE MONEY

1. **Buy used.** There are many quality resale options online for wedding-related items. Usually this is most useful for decor and/or clothes, but it can also apply to jewelry, flatware, and other physical items. Start by searching Facebook and Google.
2. **Hire a friend.** You won't get the same level of service as you would from a professional, but that can totally work as long as you set some ground rules. What do you expect this friend to do? For how long? How much will you pay them? (And yes, you should pay them at least a little because they are no longer *going* to your wedding, they are *working* your wedding.)
3. **Go DIY.** Anytime you consider DIY, first ask yourself: "What do I value more in this particular situation: my money or my time?" Be honest about what you're attempting.
4. **Invite fewer people.** Tough, I know, but also the most effective way to save money. On average, it costs $70 to feed a guest, and that's before alcohol.
5. **Host the wedding in the morning, in the winter, and/or on a weekday.** The wedding industry is highly seasonal. Use this to your advantage by picking a time that people don't always think of for weddings. You'll save money across the board.

WEDDING FUND WORKSHEET

Use this worksheet with your partner to figure out who's contributing what to your wedding. Total up the estimated amounts in the final row and see how close that number is to your estimated budget.

CONTRIBUTOR	ESTIMATED AMOUNT	SPECIFIC SERVICES OR GOODS	DO WE NEED TO REQUEST THIS MONEY? (Y/N)	IS THERE A SPECIFIC DATE THAT WE NEED THIS MONEY BY? (Y/N)	HOW WILL THIS MONEY BE SENT TO US?
US (FROM SAVINGS)					
US (FROM UPCOMING PAYCHECKS)					
VIP 1					
VIP 2					
ADDITIONAL CONTRIBUTOR 1					
ADDITIONAL CONTRIBUTOR 2					
TOTAL					

CONSIDER THIS

Planning your wedding can be an excellent opportunity to quite literally put your money where your mouth is. Hire people whose lived experiences are different from yours. Support vendors whose values align with yours. Keep it local.

OUR WEDDING BUDGET BREAKDOWN

Use your answers on the "Our Wedding Priorities" worksheet in chapter 1 (page 8) to fill out the next worksheet. Skip any vendor or item that isn't applicable. Depending on your budget, this may mean you spend zero dollars on certain services or skip them entirely.

Top Five

Spend 50 percent of your budget on these services.

_____

_____

_____

_____

Middle Five

Spend 30 percent of your budget on these services.

_____

_____

_____

_____

Bottom Five

Spend 10 percent of your budget on these services.

Non-vendor Items

Spend the remaining 10 percent of your budget on these services.

- Decorations (non-floral)
- Favors
- Gifts for VIPs
- Lighting *(if not already covered by a vendor)*
- Marriage license
- Rentals *(if not already covered by a vendor)*

3

Guest List

Deciding whom to invite to your wedding is an exercise in diplomacy. How can you possibly rank all the people you love in the world plus a few random members of your mom's book club whom she insists you invite?

Thankfully, etiquette can help. There is no way in the world that your guest list will please everyone. That would be impossible. But you can harness empathy to make sure that everyone—the invited and uninvited—feel acknowledged and cared for.

Don't believe me? Consider COVID-19. During the height of the pandemic, one of the things I heard most was relief. For couples, the pandemic had allowed them to do what, in their secret hearts, they had always wanted to do: invite fewer people.

The relief wasn't exclusive to the two people getting married. Guests were relieved, too. A false notion of good manners had trapped them into feeling they needed to go to so-and-so's wedding when, really, popping a card in the mail had always been more appropriate.

You and your partner can benefit from the lessons of that time. Ask yourselves: "Who needs to be at our wedding in person for it to feel like our wedding?" Use that question as your guiding star as you embark on one of wedding planning's most arduous tasks.

COUPLE 1

Kenji repeatedly ignored his mom's texts about a few friends she wanted to invite to his wedding. By ghosting his own relative, Kenji inadvertently made the situation worse. He missed an opportunity to have an honest but kind discussion with his mom about why she wanted to invite these people and how, perhaps, they could compromise.

COUPLE 2

Miguel and Yolanda decided to get married over a holiday. A certain family member often joined for the holiday, and while he wasn't a person Miguel or Yolanda felt particularly close to, they extended an invitation rather than exclude him.

TOP FIVE ETIQUETTE DOS

1. **Do respect The Board.** It is easy to discount what a big deal it is to the people who raised you that you're getting married. Does this mean you have to invite a bunch of people you don't care about? No. But it does mean you and your partner will be best served if you approach any conversation of "Hey, Dad, we're not inviting your fishing buddy" with warmth.

2. **Do consider other ways to include people.** Common convention is that if you invite someone to one thing, you have to invite them to everything. I disagree. Instead, I believe you can use other celebrations, like an engagement party or wedding shower, as ways to meaningfully include people as long as you're honest about what you're doing and why.

3. **Do explain your thinking (within reason).** This does not have to be a laborious process. It can be as simple as these words: "Dear Aunt Myrtle, we've decided to keep our wedding to immediate family and close friends, but we're hosting an engagement party that we'd love for you to attend."

4. **Do communicate with your guests.** If you have certain rules for your wedding, like a dress code or no kids, communicate these clearly. Make the information easy to find by putting it on a wedding website or in an invite.

5. **Do remember that you are responsible only for your own fun.** Couples often tell me that they just want their guests to have a good time. This is a worthy and noble goal. But remember that your guests are adults, too. They'll do their own thing no matter how much you may try to prevent them from doing so.

TOP FIVE ETIQUETTE DON'TS

1. **Don't shy away from virtual options (if it fits your wedding mission statement).** COVID-19 helped normalize virtual options for weddings. Use this as a nice way to invite people without expecting—or paying—for them to attend in person.

2. **Don't fear the "no kids" invite.** Don't want them at your wedding? Own it. And realize that some people you care about may have to decline because sitters are expensive. If that's a deal breaker, consider a middle option: Invite kids and hire an on-site babysitter for your wedding.

3. **Don't invite people out of pity.** Couples often tell me that more people RSVP'd yes to their wedding than they ever planned—or budgeted—to host. Please don't do this to yourself. The best option is to just not invite these people at all, but if that's not on the table, consider sending invitations in waves, starting with your VIPs and then adjusting accordingly.

4. **Don't play travel agent.** No matter how many "Things to Do" you add to your wedding website, your guests will still pull up Google Maps and go to that tourist trap restaurant. Is it nice to offer some ideas? Sure. But don't spend more than 15 minutes brainstorming.

5. **Don't feel bad if you want a big wedding.** Couples who want huge guest counts often get criticized just as much as couples who want smaller numbers. It's all just further proof that you can't make everyone happy, so do your best to satisfy yourself and your partner first.

HOW DO WE PICK?

Stuck on a guest? Try this.

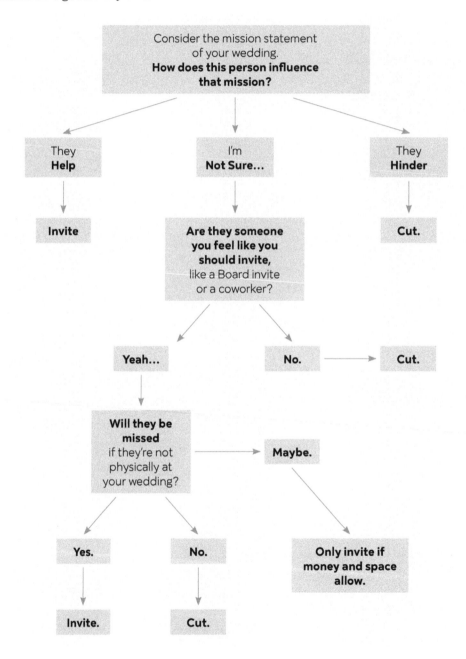

Consider the mission statement
of your wedding.
**How does this person influence
that mission?**

They
Help

I'm
Not Sure...

They
Hinder

Invite

**Are they someone
you feel like you
should invite,**
like a Board invite
or a coworker?

Cut.

Yeah...

No. → **Cut.**

**Will they be
missed**
if they're not
physically at
your wedding? → **Maybe.**

Yes.

No.

**Only invite if
money and space
allow.**

Invite.

Cut.

CONSIDER THIS

Your guests only care about two things: Where am I parking and when am I eating? Yes, they also care deeply about you and your partner, but they've probably been to a wedding before. They recognize that you two are going to be preoccupied, so as long as they're parked and fed, they'll be just fine.

WHO GETS WHAT?

Be sure to consider the following questions before making any final choices about who's invited.

- ▶ **Who gets a plus-one?** My advice: Whittle down the outer circles of guests rather than keep your inner circles from having a plus-one.
- ▶ **Are there any guests on our list for whom it would be a financial and/or physical hardship to attend our wedding in person?** If so, could they be included in a different way?
- ▶ **Are kids invited to our wedding?** If so, which ones?
- ▶ **Are pets invited to our wedding?** If so, which ones?

CONSIDER THIS

If you can swing it, hiring a shuttle or a bus is often a worthwhile expense, particularly if you're planning a wedding in a location that's hard to get to (think: rural barn) or in a spot where parking is limited (think: downtown ballroom). Bonus: A bus helps keep drunk drivers off the road.

OUR FINAL GUEST LIST

Use this space to list the names of the people invited to your wedding based on the main categories of wedding guests I often see as a planner.

These are the people who must be at our wedding in person for it to feel like our wedding.

_____   _____

_____   _____

_____   _____

_____   _____

_____   _____

_____   _____

_____   _____

_____   _____

_____   _____

_____   _____

_____   _____

_____   _____

_____   _____

_____   _____

These are the people we'd *really, really like* to be at our wedding in person.

These are the people we'd *really like* to be at our wedding in person.

_____   _____

_____   _____

_____   _____

_____   _____

_____   _____

_____   _____

_____   _____

_____   _____

_____   _____

_____   _____

_____   _____

_____   _____

_____   _____

_____   _____

_____   _____

_____   _____

_____   _____

_____   _____

These are the people we'd *like* to be at our wedding in person.

These are the *invites for The Board* we need to account for.

These are the *plus-ones* we need to account for.

_____   _____

_____   _____

_____   _____

_____   _____

_____   _____

_____   _____

_____   _____

_____   _____

_____   _____

_____   _____

_____   _____

_____   _____

_____   _____

_____   _____

_____   _____

_____   _____

_____   _____

_____   _____

These are the *kids* we need to account for.

_____   _____

_____   _____

_____   _____

_____   _____

_____   _____

_____   _____

_____   _____

_____   _____

_____   _____

_____   _____

_____   _____

_____   _____

_____   _____

_____   _____

_____   _____

_____   _____

_____   _____

_____   _____

_____   _____

WHO SITS WHERE?

While open seating may sound good, in my experience, it often backfires. You're just forcing your guests to relive that age-old dilemma of the school cafeteria where they stand, tray in hand, and look out over a sea of unfamiliar faces. So please: Just tell people where to sit. Use this exercise to help.

Follow these steps as you make your seating chart on a document outside of this book.

1. **List the top reasons you're inviting people to your wedding.** Examples include *best friend, school,* and *The Board invite.* Assign one tag to each guest member.

2. **Next, group guests by these tags.** Assign tables accordingly. If you're thinking of having round tables, create groups of six to eight. For rectangular tables, group by quartets (i.e., the people who will face each other). If you're numbering tables and those tables will be dismissed to grab food in a certain order, put VIPs at the tables that will be dismissed earlier.

Extra credit: Assign a host for each table. Provide each one a list of three to five icebreaker questions to help people discover the commonalities that inspired you to group them together. (This idea comes courtesy of experience designer Julie Comfort of The Experiential Wedding. You'll find this and other resources toward the end of the book on page 195.)

4

Venue(s)

Deciding where to host their wedding is often the first big planning decision a couple makes (besides, of course, the decision to get married at all).

As you and your partner begin the hunt, please keep the following in mind: People get married in all kinds of places. Hotels, public parks, private homes, fields without water access—I've worked weddings in all of these locations and more. Each has its pros and cons, but last I checked, nobody's marriage was more likely to succeed than anybody else's because they went with early-20th-century architecture over the rustic charm of a rural barn.

So pace yourselves and keep the mission statement of your wedding in mind. How do the venue(s) you've selected move you and your partner toward accomplishing that mission? How do they move you two away from it? Use these questions as guideposts as you begin researching, touring, and ultimately booking where you'll begin your marriage.

COUPLE 1 _____

Victor and Marco selected a renovated brick warehouse for their wedding reception. To access the dining room and dance floor, guests would first need to scale a steep 50-step staircase. No elevators or wheelchair ramps were available. The selection seriously impeded the enjoyment—and safety—of their guests and vendors.

COUPLE 2 _____

Jess and Kay were planning an 87-guest wedding at a downtown restaurant. During the venue tour, they noticed that the bathrooms were gendered. One had a sign for men, the other for women. This would make their guests feel unseen and unsafe, so they asked if the venue manager would remove the signs so the restrooms were open to any gender. The manager immediately complied.

TOP FIVE ETIQUETTE DOS

1. **Do expect homophobia, racism, and/or sexism.** Straight couples, see if the venue staff makes eye contact with the groom as frequently as they do the bride. LGBTQIA+ couples, expect to be shown spaces that are labeled "bridal suite" even if neither of you identify as a bride. This behavior is deeply disturbing and inexcusable. If you feel up to it, don't hesitate to explain—in person or online—why a venue's insensitivity inspired you to keep your money.

2. **Do consider history.** Depending on where you're planning, your options for venues may have former histories that don't align with your values (one example: plantations in the southern United States). Do your research and don't hesitate to ask a venue owner how they do—or don't—recognize the past. Consider how you and your partner can make sure not to glorify or romanticize other people's pain.

3. **Do pace yourself.** As you begin contacting venues, you'll often be asked to come in and take a tour. The tour itself is usually quite pleasant, but it takes

time. You're not obligated to get all the tours done in one single weekend. Spread them out and go together whenever possible.

4. **Do follow the rules.** Wedding venues often have lengthy contracts filled with easy-to-miss rules such as no open flames or music off by 10 p.m. Before you sign, read the fine print. These rules are there for a reason, and they're nonnegotiable.

5. **Do consider the weather.** What are your options if it rains? If it's too cold? If it's too hot? Consider these questions as you tour a venue so that you and your partner can brainstorm solutions for the actual wedding day.

TOP FIVE ETIQUETTE DON'TS

1. **Don't forget accessibility.** Is that staircase too steep for some of your guests? Where's the closest wheelchair ramp? Do the bathrooms comply with the Americans with Disabilities Act (ADA)? These things matter if you want your guests to fully enjoy themselves.

2. **Don't underestimate travel distance.** Many couples host a ceremony in one location and a reception in another. If this is your situation, be sure to factor in travel time. Is it obvious how to get from one location to another? What's parking like at each one?

3. **Don't conflate "venue coordinator" with "wedding coordinator."** The words may be used interchangeably, but they are not the same. The first is the person on-site who is responsible for the venue (think: turning on the lights and locking up). The second is a person you might hire in addition to the venue who is responsible for the flow of the wedding day.

4. **Don't forget the bathrooms.** A single stall isn't going to cut it for 100 guests. Neither is a badly lit walkway for an evening reception.

5. **Don't dismiss a weekday.** Hosting a wedding on a weekday and/or in the winter immediately makes costs drop. Your guests won't mind, either; chances are they're already taking time off work to attend.

OUR IDEAL CEREMONY WORKSHEET

A ceremony often gets skipped over because couples just want to get to the party. It's a shame because the ceremony is the beating heart of a wedding. Honor it. Use these questions to help.

1. What is our wedding's mission statement?

   _____

   _____

   _____

2. What three words best describe a ceremony that aligns with our mission statement?

   _____

3. How can we potentially incorporate the activities that we like to do together as a couple into our wedding ceremony?

   _____

   _____

   _____

4. What are we each afraid of happening during our ceremony?

   ◆ Partner 1

   _____

   _____

- Partner 2

_____

5. What are we each most looking forward to happening during our ceremony?

   - Partner 1

   _____

   - Partner 2

   _____

6. During our ceremony, how do we want our guests to feel?

   _____

7. During our ceremony, how do we want to feel?

   _____

BOOKING A VENUE

Use these yes/no questions to help you and your partner sort through your venue options. Hint: The most important question is at the end.

Does this venue fall within our budget?   [Yes / No]

If we have a particular date that we want, is the venue available?   [Yes / No]

Will this venue fit our current guest count?   [Yes / No]

Is this venue accessible to all our guests? Is it safe for them?   [Yes / No]

Does this venue include any amenities that we have identified as a priority for our wedding? (For example, indoor restrooms, in-house catering, access to tables, chairs, and other rentals.)   [Yes / No]

Does the venue's availability on the day before our wedding and the day of our wedding align with our goals? (This question matters because some venues have strict windows of time when you can access the space for rehearsals, setup, and cleanup.)   [Yes / No]

Does the venue require anything extra from us, such as event liability insurance or liquor liability insurance?   [Yes / No]

Does the venue have parking?   [Yes / No]

Will this venue move us closer to our mission statement?   [Yes / No]

CONSIDER THIS

If you're hosting a ceremony and a reception in the same location, you may hear the word "flip." This means changing a room from a ceremony layout to a reception layout. Talk to the venue contact about who handles the flip and the timing. Will you and your guests be expected to leave? For how long?

OUR IDEAL RECEPTION WORKSHEET

A reception is a party, but it's also a way for your community to recognize the start of your marriage. Consider what that means as you fill this out together.

1. What is the mission statement of our wedding?

    ....

    ....

    ....

2. What three words best describe a reception that aligns with our mission statement?

    ....

3. How can we potentially incorporate the activities that we like to do together as a couple into our wedding ceremony?

    ....

    ....

    ....

4. What are we afraid of happening during our reception?

    ◆ Partner 1

    ....

    ◆ Partner 2

    ....

5. What are we most looking forward to happening during our reception?

♦ Partner 1

....

....

♦ Partner 2

....

....

6. During our reception, how do we want our guests to feel?

....

....

....

7. During our reception, how do we want to feel?

....

....

....

VENUE: MUST-ASK QUESTIONS

1. When can we get in on the day of?

2. When do we need to be out?

3. How is the space usually laid out for a wedding?

4. Who is the venue's contact for the wedding day?

5. When can we have our rehearsal? (This may very well *not* be the day before the wedding.)

6. Who provides what? (Does the venue provide chairs, tables, linens, plates, utensils, glasses, and/or A/V, or will you need to arrange for those items separately?)

7. Where does the trash, recycling, and compost go? (You—or someone you hire, such as a caterer—may be responsible.)

8. Is there anything we need to keep in mind for the end of the night? (Examples include an early shutoff time for music and particular rules for cleanup.)

9. What's the parking situation?

10. What's the insurance situation?

11. Who's doing the floor plan?

12. Does the venue only work with certain vendors, or can we hire anyone we want?

13. Are there any fees for bringing in our own alcohol (if applicable)?

14. Is there anything we didn't ask that we should have?

CONSIDER THIS

Depending on where in the world you're looking for venues, your options may be limited when it comes to sustainability. While touring, ask about composting, recycling, and other ways that the venue prioritizes the environment. If you hit a dead end, brainstorm more ways these needs could be met.

COMPARING VENUES

NAME OF VENUE	VENUE CONTACT	LOCATION	AVAILABLE FOR OUR DATE?	PRICE

CONSIDER THIS

Your venue may require that you buy event liability insurance, potentially with liquor liability included. If you have other insurance, talk to your agent. Your venue may also recommend websites like The Event Helper, WedSafe, and Travelers Insurance. Note that event liability insurance is different from cancellation insurance, which is a separate (and more uncommon) purchase.

OUR WEDDING VENUE(S)

Our venue(s) are:

_____

_____

_____

_____

HOURS	ACCESSIBLE FOR OUR GUESTS? (Y/N)	CEREMONY, RECEPTION, BOTH?	ADDITIONAL NOTES	TOP THREE PROS	TOP THREE CONS	OVERALL RATING (1 TO 5)

This is what our venue(s) cost and when that money is due:

This is what our venue(s) provide:

This is when we can get into our venue(s):

_____

_____

_____

_____

_____

This is information about our venue(s) that we need to mention to our guests:

_____

_____

_____

_____

_____

This is information about our venue(s) that we need to mention to our vendors:

_____

_____

_____

_____

_____

This is when our final walk-through will likely occur at our venue(s):

These are other details that we want to remember:

SELECTING OUR OFFICIANT

	NAME(S) AND PRONOUNS	CONTACT INFORMATION	AVAILABLE FOR OUR WEDDING? (Y/N)	AVAILABLE FOR OUR REHEARSAL (AS APPLICABLE)? (Y/N)
OFFICIANT 1				
OFFICIANT 2				
OFFICIANT 3				

OFFICIANT: MUST-ASK QUESTIONS

1. Are you legally qualified to marry us?

2. *If you are hiring*: Why do you want to marry us?

3. *If you are asking a loved one to officiate*: Do you feel comfortable taking on this responsibility?

4. *If your officiant has done this before*: What is one thing you learned from your previous experiences that we should keep in mind for our wedding?

5. *If your officiant hasn't done this before*: What is one thing you are nervous about for our wedding day, and how could we help support you?

6. Who will write our ceremony script? Our vows?

7. Do we want to include a land acknowledgment? (*A land acknowledgment is a formal statement that respects and recognizes the past and present relationship specific Indigenous peoples have to an area and should be handled with the utmost care.*)

8. Do we want to recognize anyone who couldn't physically be with us?

FEE	STYLE/TONE	TOP THREE PROS	TOP THREE CONS	OVERALL RATING (1 TO 5)

9. If we are having a rehearsal, will you be able to attend?

10. Do you need anything printed out before our wedding?

11. What will this service cost?

12. Is there anything we should have asked but didn't?

5

Invitations

Booking a venue immediately makes your wedding feel more real. You now have a time and a place to point to and say, "On this day at this location, I am marrying the person I love." That is huge, and I hope you and your partner take a moment for a celebratory dance party!

Afterward, let's continue to tighten the focus on the blurry outline of Project Wedding Day. We've got the where. We've got the when. Now we need the who.

You and your partner probably already have a good idea of who's invited thanks to your work in chapter 3 to develop a guest list. Of course, you made that guest list and then promptly forgot about it in the hustle and bustle of finding a venue. That's okay! You still have plenty of time to tell people about your wedding.

That's where invites come in. Like so much of wedding planning, communicating with your guests can be as complicated as you want it to be. The trick is to remember that your wedding will never matter as much to your guests as it does to you and your partner.

That sounds cold, but it's actually a relief. You can feel a strong sense of urgency to make sure everybody knows about everything when in reality, your guests need very little information in order to fully enjoy themselves. Let's help them, shall we?

COUPLE 1

Jamie made the ultimate error with their guests: They contacted them too often. Rather than direct guests to one or two points of communication, Jamie regularly texted, DM'd, and emailed guests updates about their wedding. The result was mass confusion. Guests couldn't keep the details straight!

COUPLE 2

Liam and Amir dedicated a tab on their wedding website to accessibility. They provided their guests with pertinent information about how to access their venue, including what guests could expect in terms of layout, terrain, and accommodations. Only a small percentage of their guests needed these details to fully enjoy the day, but all appreciated the information.

TOP FIVE ETIQUETTE DOS

1. **Do cover the basics.** Make it easy and create one resource (e.g., a website, a Facebook group, an invitation) where you can send curious guests.

2. **Do talk about attire.** Usually this means two or three adjectives on a guest-facing correspondence that describe the tone of the wedding ("black tie," "family dinner," "casual picnic"). Bonus points if you mention shoes ("We're getting married in a field, so skip the stilettos").

3. **Do ask for everything you need in one correspondence.** There's a chance that you and your partner may need to collect information about your guests such as food allergies, plus-ones, kids, and other safety details (a modern example: COVID-19 vaccination status). Ask for this information early and all at once rather than hit your guests with multiple messages that they'll only lose track of.

4. **Do register.** One of the ways that people show love is by gift-giving. Don't deny your guests this opportunity. I also encourage you to ask for things you and your partner actually want—including cash. Many registries offer tasteful options that allow guests to contribute toward an experience; other registries allow donations to nonprofits you and your partner support.

5. **Do expect people to forget.** No matter how effective the communication plan is for your wedding, people will still text you the day before and ask, "When is the ceremony again?" Have a message drafted that you can copy and paste, and remember: They're adults. They'll figure it out.

TOP FIVE ETIQUETTE DON'TS

1. **Don't fall into the trap of inviting everyone to everything.** The go-to advice of "if you invite someone to one thing, you have to invite them to all things" is antiquated and impractical. It's also, ironically, not inclusive, because often someone can better afford to go to one event rather than all events. As such, it's okay to invite a favorite girlfriend to a bridal shower but not the wedding. Just tell her that's the case: "We're keeping the wedding day small, but it was important to me to celebrate this transition with you."

2. **Don't spend hours on your wedding website.** There are many premade, nice-looking, free templates. Use them. Don't waste time on a website unless, of course, website development brings you joy (and for some it does).

3. **Don't expect people to RSVP on time.** They won't, so set your public-facing RSVP deadline a week ahead of when you actually need RSVPs. This will help reduce the inevitable list of calls and texts you'll need to send to track down late responders.

4. **Don't discount digital.** Sending an e-vite is not tacky. Indeed, it's often the most efficient option, particularly if you're collecting a lot of information. The biggest downside is that you won't be supporting a local small business, so consider hiring a printmaker to create collateral like signs, menus, or programs.

5. **Don't overcomplicate.** When it's time to send invites, do it all in one go, ideally as an assembly line where you and your partner each handle one or two tasks. This may take a few hours, but it's much more efficient.

WEDDING WEBSITE

A wedding website can be an extremely useful tool when it comes to informing your guests. It's also an accessible one thanks to a wide variety of free options (the cost is usually your email address, which prompts a whole slew of emails from which I recommend you promptly unsubscribe).

Of course, a website can also become a total time-suck. Couples may labor for hours over writing the perfect "About Us" section or the ideal bio for every VIP. These details are lovely—and completely unnecessary.

So keep it simple. Cover the basics. Make the most valuable information the easiest to find. When in doubt, default to the five Ws and one H (who, what, where, when, why, and how). Remember that your guests have likely been to a wedding before. They have a general idea of what to expect; what they need from you are your particular expectations for this particular wedding.

WHAT TO INCLUDE ON OUR WEDDING WEBSITE

- ☐ **Who is getting married?**
- ☐ **What is happening?**
- ☐ **Where is this happening?** Include what's indoors and what's outdoors.
- ☐ **When is this happening?** Include the date and the ceremony start time. Other timings are important but will be shared later with the necessary VIPs.
- ☐ **Why is this happening?** This is where you can share some of your story as a couple.
- ☐ **How is this happening?** Consider parking, hotel recommendations, room block information, shuttle details, attire descriptions, on-site babysitting information, and any unexpected costs your guests should expect, like parking fees or toll roads.
- ☐ **How to RSVP.**
- ☐ **Accessibility and safety.** Does the venue have a steep staircase? Is there a long walk between locations? What's the terrain like?
- ☐ **Your registry.**
- ☐ **A thank-you.** To show appreciation for your guests' time, effort, love, and support.
- ☐ **VIPs** (optional). Who they are, how they know you, and their role in the wedding.
- ☐ **Photos** (optional).

CONSIDER THIS

Registering doesn't necessarily mean you have to choose a big-box retailer or ask for bargain items. It's okay to ask for things that will set your marriage up for success. Many registries also offer ways for guests to contribute a portion of their choosing toward a big-ticket item—a nice option for a wide range of budgets.

SAVE-THE-DATE

The goal of a save-the-date is to get you and your partner on certain people's calendars so that they don't accidentally double-book. As such, a save-the-date has minimal information. It's often a single date, a general location, and maybe a URL to a wedding website. The most important details—ceremony start time, venue address, registry—come later.

Sending a save-the-date can be useful, particularly if you're getting married during a time of year when people often vacation or may have other weddings to attend. Sending one can also be redundant since the people who must be at your wedding for it to feel like your wedding usually already know the details—because, well, they're VIPs!

If you've covered the bases, great. You can turn down the dial on the save-the-date pressure cooker. Consider sending save-the-dates if they're the most effective way to get on calendars and if they're in budget. Don't send them if you've already accomplished that goal or if they're not in budget.

What would you do instead? Options include bcc'd emails, phone calls, group text messages, or a Facebook group. Remember what you're trying to accomplish and let that dictate how you do it.

SAVE-THE-DATES: MUST-HAVE DETAILS

▸ **Who is getting married.**
▸ **The date of the wedding.** Do not include the dates for any other wedding-related activities such as a rehearsal dinner or post-wedding brunch. That information will come later.

- ▸ **The general location of the wedding.** A city and state (or country) is great. Give people ample time to budget and book travel, as needed.
- ▸ **A wedding website.** This can totally come later, if it's applicable at all, but if you have one ready, put the URL on the save-the-date. This gives people a way to educate themselves instead of relying on you for all information.
- ▸ **A heads-up if you're also sending an invite.** Often this is worded as "Invitation to follow."
- ▸ **Rarely, an RSVP.** Honestly, if your headcount is that tight, rethink your guest list.

CONSIDER THIS

When do you send all these things? For save-the-dates, aim for five to eight months before the wedding. Plan to send your invites six weeks to three months before the wedding. Don't sweat the schedule too much unless you're asking guests to travel internationally. Your most important guests probably already know all about the wedding.

INVITATIONS

Your invite is the biggest and perhaps only piece of guest-facing communication that you and your partner will send about your wedding. Thankfully, it's pretty hard to mess up.

In its purest form, an invite includes the when and where of a wedding plus an RSVP deadline. This means figuring out when your wedding starts (we'll discuss how to do this in chapter 12), where your wedding is happening (already done!), and when you need answers back (likely three to four weeks before the wedding).

From here, you can add as much or as little information as you and your partner want. Less is often better because, as we've already established, people get confused easily.

Word count may also be limited, so include the URL for a wedding website where you'll have an FAQ page. If you're skipping a website, no problem. Just expect to write more on the invite. Give precedence to the most vital information.

CONSIDER THIS

We've all seen the invites that list the names of the people paying for the wedding (i.e., The Board). Do you need to do this? Nowadays, the answer is no. But do recognize these people in another way, perhaps with a toast at the wedding or in a private thank-you card.

INVITATIONS: MUST-HAVE DETAILS

- ▶ **Who is getting married.**
- ▶ **The date of the wedding.**
- ▶ **The specific location(s) of the wedding.** Include any addresses and, as needed, more specific directions in case online directions are confusing.
- ▶ **How and when to RSVP.** The actual RSVP might be a separate piece of paper, or it might be a link to an RSVP form online. Make the deadline clear.
- ▶ **A wedding website.** No website? No problem. List this information on the invite directly.
- ▶ **A sense of what to expect.** Examples include "there will be a post-ceremony dessert buffet" or "dinner and dancing to follow."
- ▶ **Details about attire.**

You do NOT need to include information about pre- or post-wedding activities unless those activities are open to all guests. If they're not (and usually they're not), keep this invite specific to the wedding.

6

Wedding Day Attire

It's unlikely you will ever give any outfit as much thought as you do the outfit you wear to your wedding. Some of this is pressure we put on ourselves. Much of it comes from others. Can you think of any other clothing decision that has spawned so many reality TV shows and pithy catchphrases?

Complicating matters further is the reality that you will likely be selecting your outfit by committee. You may even be telling other adult people what to wear. This can be an uncomfortable fit, so do your best to remember what you wrote down in the "Wedding Vision Worksheet" in chapter 1 (page 5). How do you want to feel on your wedding day?

Keep the answer to that question close as you begin shopping, because what we wear often influences how we feel. And how you feel is the most important thing when it comes to your wedding. Say yes to whatever feeling you want, and the rest will follow.

COUPLE 1

Angel had always wanted to wear a black wedding dress, but their sister insisted the idea was "just not done." Angel violated their own boundary and went with a white dress even though they knew it was more their sister's style than their own. They always regretted it.

COUPLE 2

Rather than require her VIPs to get the exact same outfit, Michelle recognized that each of her friends had a unique body and budget. She offered a specific selection of colors, cuts, and costs and let her friends select what worked—and looked—best for them.

TOP FIVE ETIQUETTE DOS

1. **Do consider custom.** The word "custom" may have you seeing dollar signs, but in many cases, working with a designer is actually the same cost (or even cheaper) than buying off the rack. That's because your outfit is specifically tailored for you, so you don't end up owing for alterations or tailoring.

2. **Do honor family heirlooms.** Grandma's veil probably has a lot of meaning even if Grandma herself had questionable taste. Respect the intent of the offer and approach any refusal with warmth and creativity. Could the veil be incorporated in another way without you wearing the darn thing all day?

3. **Do help your guests help themselves.** If you and your partner are hosting a wedding that features cultural traditions that may not be familiar to some of your guests, help them know what is and isn't okay. For example, if some guests are wearing saris, would it be appropriate for all guests to do the same? Tell them.

4. **Do dress for comfort.** Your wedding day is a marathon. Rather than end up barefoot halfway during your reception, pick shoes you can actually stand to wear for more than an hour. Or, if you like nothing more than going barefoot, do so!

5. **Do know what you're asking.** Dress code terms like "black tie," "white tie," and even "dressy casual" all have different meanings to different people. If you have something very specific in mind, provide examples.

TOP FIVE ETIQUETTE DON'TS

1. **Don't expect everyone to like what you pick.** They won't. You know your style best, so rather than spam your friends with endless photos of outfits, go with your gut. Which outfit makes you feel most like yourself?

2. **Don't assume anything.** What's a bargain for you may not be the same for a VIP. Where possible, offer a range of options. If there's something you particularly want, like a certain accessory, buy it yourself and offer it as a gift.

3. **Don't appropriate.** When in doubt, google. What is the significance of this item, and what about that significance speaks so strongly to you? Is there another way you can satisfy that desire while also respecting the boundaries of the culture in question?

4. **Don't shame your guests—or yourself.** What we put on our bodies is a deeply personal choice. If you don't like what someone wears to your wedding, please keep it to yourself. Take that kindness and apply it to yourself, too. Many people often feel compelled to look a certain way always and especially on their wedding day. Be gentle and ask yourself whom that crash diet serves. Is it you?

5. **Don't hesitate to set limits.** If you feel yourself already sweating at the thought of an entourage, honor that instinct. Either limit who joins you or go alone. This will likely buck the norm, so explain to your important person or people who thought they were joining you: "I'd love to do a little research before we pick my dress. I'd like to go shopping and then send you a few photos to get your opinion."

MY OUTFIT INSPIRATION WORKSHEET

What's my favorite outfit ever?

....

....

Are there elements of that outfit that I'd like to include in the outfit I wear to my wedding?

....

....

If I could wear anything in the world to my wedding, what would it be and why?

....

....

What are three adjectives I would use to describe this ideal outfit?

....

What are three adjectives I would like other people to use to describe what I wear to my wedding?

....

Who am I dressing for on my wedding day?

....

....

How do I want my wedding day outfit to make that person (or people) feel?

How do I want my wedding day outfit to make me feel?

What is my ideal budget for this outfit? (Consider all elements, including accessories and undergarments.)

What are some places I think I can find this outfit? (Include any elements you might be able to source from loved ones, resale shops, online outlets, etc.)

KEEPING TRACK OF YOUR CANDIDATES

OPTIONS	WHERE I FOUND IT	COST	WILL IT NEED ALTERATIONS OR TAILORING?	THREE THINGS I LIKE	THREE THINGS I DON'T LIKE	OVERALL RATING (1 TO 5)

THE WINNER

This is what I'm wearing to our wedding:

_____

_____

_____

This is what my wedding outfit costs:

_____

These are the places where I'm finding all parts of my wedding outfit:

_____

_____

_____

_____

This is the work I may still need to do to complete my wedding outfit (include dates for fittings, alterations, tailoring, etc.):

_____

_____

_____

_____

This is the date I'll have my wedding outfit done and with me:

_____

These are other details I want to remember:

_____

_____

_____

_____

CONSIDER THIS

The usual advice is to start shopping for wedding day attire eight to ten months before your wedding. This is useful because of how long alterations and tailoring may take, but don't fret if your hunt starts a little later. You're in good shape as long as you're researching your options early.

MY PARTNER'S INSPIRATION WORKSHEET

What's my favorite outfit ever?

_____

_____

Are there elements of that outfit that I'd like to include in the outfit I wear to
my wedding?

_____

_____

_____

If I could wear anything in the world to my wedding, what would it be and why?

_____

_____

_____

What are three adjectives I would use to describe this ideal outfit?

_____

What are three adjectives I would like other people to use to describe what I wear
to my wedding?

_____

Who am I dressing for on my wedding day?

_____

_____

_____

How do I want my wedding day outfit to make that person (or people) feel?

How do I want my wedding day outfit to make me feel?

What is my ideal budget for this outfit? (Consider all elements, including accessories and undergarments.)

What are some places I think I can find this outfit? (Include any elements you might be able to source from loved ones, resale shops, online outlets, etc.)

KEEPING TRACK OF THE CANDIDATES

OPTIONS	WHERE I FOUND IT	COST	WILL IT NEED ALTERATIONS OR TAILORING?	THREE THINGS I LIKE	THREE THINGS I DON'T LIKE	OVERALL RATING (1 TO 5)

THE WINNER

This is what I'm wearing to our wedding:

_____

_____

This is what my wedding outfit costs:

_____

This is the work I may still need to do to complete my wedding outfit (include dates for fittings, alterations, tailoring, etc.):

_____

_____

_____

This is when I'll have my wedding outfit done and with me:

....

These are other details I want to remember:

....

....

....

....

RENTING VS. BUYING

At first glance, the idea of renting your wedding day outfit can seem sacrilegious. Isn't this an outfit you're supposed to keep forever in the back of your closet and/or pay to preserve for eternity?

For some people, the answer is yes. For others, the answer is no. Wherever you fall on the spectrum, make your choice based on what you personally want to do with these clothes after you wear them—not out of a fear that renting is cheap or abnormal. It's not!

Unfortunately, however, it can be quite hard to rent depending on what type of outfit we're talking about. Many quality rental options for wedding dresses have gone bust in recent years, which means that you may be better served by buying pre-owned. Thankfully, there are loads of top-notch consignment options for wedding dresses. Suits, tuxes, and bridesmaids' dresses remain relatively easy to rent.

As you research, keep an eye on when rental items are due back. There's a chance it may be the day after your wedding, which might be a busy one. Save yourself a last-minute headache and arrange for a trusted person to handle the return. Also note if the item needs to be cleaned before it's sent back (unlikely).

ACCESSORIZE

There are many options for wedding day accessories. Keep flowers in mind if you're planning on having any. They can serve as accessories, too.

- ► Belts and sashes (both for dresses and for pants)
- ► Cape, jacket, or wrap (might be useful depending on the time of day and season)
- ► Hair accessory and/or headwear (barrettes, clips, tiaras, hats, etc.)
- ► Garter (interest may vary)
- ► Gloves
- ► Jewelry (earrings, tie clips, lapel pins, necklaces, bracelets, watches, rings, cufflinks, etc.)
- ► Shoes (opt for comfort!)
- ► Socks (tip: socks can make a nice, affordable gift for VIPs)
- ► Pj's (some couples opt for a special night-of outfit)
- ► Purse or going-away bag
- ► Ties and/or pocket squares
- ► Traditional clothing and/or family heirlooms
- ► Undergarments (consider the cut of your outfit)
- ► Veil (multiple lengths and fabric types available)

HAIR, MAKEUP, NAILS, AND MORE

Start by prioritizing what you and your partner want. Then, budget permitting, consider using beauty and grooming as a way to thank certain people (e.g., treat your stepmother-in-law to a mani-pedi the week of your wedding). Use these questions to brainstorm.

What is a beauty and grooming activity that we each indulge in when we want to treat ourselves?

Is there a special beauty and grooming activity that we each want to make sure we do before or on our wedding day?

_____

_____

_____

_____

Are there any beauty and grooming activities that we want to participate in with others?

_____

_____

_____

_____

CONSIDER THIS

Be clear about what you are and aren't paying for, and don't shy away from sharing prices if, for example, you're hiring a stylist but would like each VIP to cover their particular treatment. What's rude is when you aren't honest and your maid of honor finds herself paying for something she didn't expect.

BEAUTY AND GROOMING: THE FINAL PLAN

Partner 1

This is what I'm doing on our wedding day for beauty and grooming:

This is what it will cost:

These are other details I want to remember. (Examples include when treatments start, if your hair needs to be wet or dry, if you're sourcing any particular products, etc.)

Partner 2

This is what I'm doing on our wedding day for beauty and grooming:

This is what it will cost:

These are other details I want to remember. (Examples include when treatments start, if your hair needs to be wet or dry, if you're sourcing any particular products, etc.)

Together

This is what we're expecting VIPs to do on our wedding day for beauty and grooming:

This is what it will cost and who is contributing what:

These are other details we need to share with VIPs:

_____

_____

_____

_____

THE RINGS

If you and/or your partner are planning to wear a ring to symbolize your marriage, you can source them from any number of places—family, the internet, or a local jeweler. You can even make your own!

As you plan, think about how you want to feel every time you look at your ring. Is there a particular color, cut, jewel, and/or design that will evoke a particular feeling? How was your ring made? Is that jewel conflict-free? Is that metal responsibly mined, eco-friendly, recycled? (Look for the designation "Fairmined.")

OPTIONS	WHERE I FOUND IT	COST	TO BE RESIZED? (Y/N)	WHEN WILL IT BE READY?	THREE THINGS I LIKE	THREE THINGS I DON'T LIKE	OVERALL RATING (1 TO 5)

RING WINNERS

Partner 1

This is the ring I'm buying for our wedding:

This is what my ring costs:

This is when I'll have my ring done and with me:

These are other details I want to remember:

Partner 2

This is the ring I'm buying for our wedding:

This is what my ring costs:

This is when I'll have my ring done and with me:

These are other details I want to remember:

7

The Wedding Party (aka Our VIPs)

Do you have to have a wedding party? Of course not, but having people witness your wedding is one of the few required elements. Depending on where you're getting married, you'll likely need at least one and maybe two witnesses to sign your marriage license. In many cases, that means you'll have a wedding party of some sort, and choosing who makes up that party can be an emotionally fraught decision.

The wedding party is the inner circle. These are the VIPs whom you and your partner have chosen to play some role in the creation of your marriage. By picking them for this responsibility, you're asking them to do specified things including, but not limited to, wearing certain clothes, attending certain functions, and doing certain activities, like signing the license or giving a toast.

How do you even begin to choose your wedding party? Leaning on etiquette can help ensure nobody—including you—gets hurt.

Remember the mission statement of your wedding. Be honest with yourselves about who will help you most effectively in fulfilling that mission, and who will hinder you. Then keep the Golden Rule in mind as you share who is and isn't a part of the party. If the roles were reversed, how would you want to be told?

COUPLE 1

Karla and Tiara had never felt particularly close to Karla's sister, Krista. The etiquette error wasn't in *not* including Krista as a bridesmaid; that was the couple's choice and they were right to prioritize other loved ones. The error was in not finding some small way to recognize Krista's role in their lives such as a thank-you note, flower arrangement, or other role in the ceremony or reception.

COUPLE 2

Trang had two childhood best friends whom she considered sisters. Rather than "pick a favorite," she decided to make both her maids of honor. She spoke with each woman to figure out what this role would look like in the wedding and then assigned responsibilities accordingly.

TOP FIVE ETIQUETTE DOS

1. **Do watch your language.** Many of the default words we use in weddings are inherently gendered. Ask your VIPs what they want to be called and share those choices with your guests and vendors so everyone can work together to make people feel seen and safe.

2. **Do think outside the box.** There are many ways to acknowledge someone's significance in your life without making them an official VIP. Ask them to do a reading or give a toast. Buy them flowers to wear at the wedding, write them a private thank-you note, and/or highlight them in a speech of your own.

3. **Do consider money.** As soon as you ask someone to be a VIP, you're asking them to make a financial commitment, usually in the form of clothing, hair/makeup, and/or travel. Keep this in mind before you ask, and, as much as possible, communicate what you are and aren't expecting your party to pay for so they can budget accordingly.

4. **Do skip any role that doesn't serve you.** As long as you've got your bases covered on the legal number of witnesses, nobody else is required. This includes the roles often filled by children, such as flower girls or ring bearers (fun fact: these roles are just as easily played by adults).

5. **Do let them bring a buddy.** Yes, it will add to your guest count, but letting your VIPs have a plus-one is a small way you can thank them for all the work they've put into your wedding.

TOP FIVE ETIQUETTE DON'TS

1. **Don't ask everyone.** If you have too many people accompanying you at your ceremony, it can become unmanageable to choose outfits or schedule pre-wedding festivities. Wherever possible, err on the side of smaller and don't feel obligated to have the same number of people for each partner.

2. **Don't feel confined by tradition.** A wedding party is meant to be a collection of people you love best in the world who had a specific hand in helping you and your partner thrive as a couple. Honor that definition as you ask people. Only use tradition as it serves your mission.

3. **Don't assume they want to give a toast.** Ask before you assign and give any speech-giver plenty of warning. Also consider offering an opportunity to speak that's not as high-pressure as a reception (a rehearsal dinner or other pre-wedding festivity works well).

4. **Don't worry about ushers, pages, or train bearers unless you need them.** These roles are often from a different age. Only use them if you need them. For example, ushers might be useful if you have guests who require assistance to get to their spots.

5. **Don't think people aren't wondering.** For better or worse, people care about who "makes the cut." If there's someone you strongly considered but who didn't make the cut, recognize them in a different way. This is particularly useful for relatives.

HOW TO ASK

Just ask. This advice runs counter to much of what you may have read elsewhere, as how to ask has turned into somewhat of a cottage industry. If custom gifts and monogrammed robes are your style, go for it. If not, skip without shame. Nobody's expecting a prize. Indeed, the ask is often what people value most.

When you do ask, it can be nice to share why you made this choice. Why are you asking this particular person to witness the start of your marriage? What role do they play in your life? What role do they play in your relationship with your partner?

Also try to ask everyone within the same window of time. People talk, and you want to make sure no one accidentally gets their feelings hurt because of a lag in communication.

Later, after the emotional dust has settled, regroup with your VIPs to discuss specifics such as what they can expect to pay and to do. The more time you can give someone to plan and budget, the better. You've just promoted these loved ones from "wedding guest" to "wedding VIP." The more you can set expectations for that role, the more everyone—including you and your partner—will be able to enjoy the actual wedding.

CONSIDER THIS

Is it rude to demote a VIP? Yes, but that doesn't mean you shouldn't do it. If someone is actively detracting from the joy you and your partner are feeling for the start of your marriage, it's imperative that you ask them to step away.

OUR VIPS

Partner 1's VIP(s)

- **Name:** ....
- Pronouns: ....
- Role in wedding: ....
- Phone: ....
- Email: ....
- **Name:** ....
- Pronouns: ....
- Role in wedding: ....
- Phone: ....
- Email: ....
- **Name:** ....
- Pronouns: ....
- Role in wedding: ....
- Phone: ....
- Email: ....
- **Name:** ....
- Pronouns: ....
- Role in wedding: ....
- Phone: ....
- Email: ....

- ◆ **Name:** ....
- ◆ Pronouns: ....
- ◆ Role in wedding: ....
- ◆ Phone: ....
- ◆ Email: ....
- ◆ **Name:** ....
- ◆ Pronouns: ....
- ◆ Role in wedding: ....
- ◆ Phone: ....
- ◆ Email: ....
- ◆ **Name:** ....
- ◆ Pronouns: ....
- ◆ Role in wedding: ....
- ◆ Phone: ....
- ◆ Email: ....
- ◆ **Name:** ....
- ◆ Pronouns: ....
- ◆ Role in wedding: ....
- ◆ Phone: ....
- ◆ Email: ....

Partner 2's VIP(s)

- ◆ **Name:** ....
- ◆ Pronouns: ....
- ◆ Role in wedding: ....

- ◆ Phone: ....
- ◆ Email: ....
- ◆ **Name:** ....
- ◆ Pronouns: ....
- ◆ Role in wedding: ....
- ◆ Phone: ....
- ◆ Email: ....
- ◆ **Name:** ....
- ◆ Pronouns: ....
- ◆ Role in wedding: ....
- ◆ Phone: ....
- ◆ Email: ....
- ◆ **Name:** ....
- ◆ Pronouns: ....
- ◆ Role in wedding: ....
- ◆ Phone: ....
- ◆ Email: ....
- ◆ **Name:** ....
- ◆ Pronouns: ....
- ◆ Role in wedding: ....
- ◆ Phone: ....
- ◆ Email: ....
- ◆ **Name:** ....
- ◆ Pronouns: ....

- ◆ Role in wedding: ....
- ◆ Phone: ....
- ◆ Email: ....
- ◆ **Name:** ....
- ◆ Pronouns: ....
- ◆ Role in wedding: ....
- ◆ Phone: ....
- ◆ Email: ....
- ◆ **Name:** ....
- ◆ Pronouns: ....
- ◆ Role in wedding: ....
- ◆ Phone: ....
- ◆ Email: ....

CONSIDER THIS

Do you and/or your partner want any pre-wedding festivities such as a wedding shower, bridal shower, and/or bachelor or bachelorette party? If so, ask for these. Be clear on who's planning what so your loved ones don't have to scramble.

CONSIDER THIS

Don't forget to pick the person or people who will sign your legal marriage license. They don't have to be official VIPs to witness your ceremony. How many witnesses you need will depend on where you're getting married. Also be sure to review certain requirements, such as any minimum age for the witness(es).

VIP ATTIRE

One of the best things you can do for any VIP is to be clear on what you want them to wear. If the answer is "We don't care," that's totally fine. But do offer one to three adjectives about what you two will be wearing. This will save you a lot of frantic texts.

VIPs	WHAT ARE THEY WEARING?	COST (BE SPECIFIC ON WHO'S PAYING FOR WHAT; "THEY'RE PAYING FOR EVERYTHING" IS 100 PERCENT OKAY)	WILL IT NEED ALTERATIONS OR TAILORING? (Y/N)

WILL THE OUTFIT BE READY IN TIME FOR THIS PERSON'S TRAVEL TO THE WEDDING?	DO THEY NEED ANY-THING FROM US TO FINALIZE THEIR CHOICE?	ARE WE PROVIDING ANY-THING (E.G., JEWELRY, TIES, SOCKS, ETC.)?	ARE THERE ANY POR-TIONS THAT WE WILL NEED TO RETURN ON THIS PERSON'S BEHALF?

8

Photography, Music, Food, and More

As we begin this next section, please keep in mind that you've already booked the only required wedding vendor: the officiant. All other vendors—wedding planner, photographer, DJ, caterer, etc.—provide valuable, important services. But they are not required for your wedding (or your marriage) to be a success.

Start by referring to previous chapters to remind yourself of the guidelines that you and your partner set in the early days of planning your wedding. What is the mission statement of your wedding? What vendors did you identify as the most important to accomplishing this mission? How much money do you have to spend on this team?

The answers to these questions form the outline of your hiring plan. Now start to fill in the blanks. Because you've done the hard work of prioritizing what you and your partner want, now's the time to let loose and recruit the team to execute your truly excellent party!

While planning this party, do not feel restrained by convention or what you've seen in magazines or on TV. If those images serve the mission statement of your wedding, by all means, let them inspire you.

If they don't, explore what serves you two better. Chances are good you can find someone to make that dream come true, because wedding vendors are in the business of joy. They want you to be happy, and they're thrilled when you want the same.

COUPLE 1

While planning their wedding, Farah and Omar dedicated themselves to their checklists. Soon, however, their priority became checking off an item rather than asking themselves if—and why—they wanted the item at all. The result was a stressful and impersonal planning experience (and more than one fight).

COUPLE 2

Jenna and Elena were not cake people. Rather than force themselves to eat a dessert they felt no connection to, they decided to rent an ice cream truck to come to their wedding reception. The result was a showstopping surprise that was in line with their values as a couple.

TOP FIVE ETIQUETTE DOS

1. **Do look for yourselves.** When hiring any vendor—and particularly a vendor who offers a more aesthetic service such as hair, makeup, photography, or videography—look for yourself and your partner in that person's gallery of work. Do they celebrate and cherish working with couples who look like you and your partner? Does their work recognize joy that isn't only between white, straight, cis, skinny people who don't live with visible disabilities?

2. **Do read reviews and sign contracts.** If third-party reviews are scarce, ask for referrals. If you decide to hire someone, require a contract—even and particularly if that person is a friend.

3. **Do be clear about what you're buying.** This is especially important if you're trying to figure out a more affordable way to accomplish a certain task. For example, if catering for your wedding will be a family-provided potluck, who's washing the dishes? These questions have easy answers as long as you ask them well in advance.

4. **Do consider yourself an employer.** You aren't just putting together a random collection of people. You're hiring a team. Treat your vendors like you would want to be treated by your own boss. Respect the power you have in this relationship.

5. **Do talk about your family.** Be honest with your vendors about any challenging dynamics that exist between VIPs. Are there two people who really shouldn't be put next to each other? Tell your team.

TOP FIVE ETIQUETTE DON'TS

1. **Don't hesitate to ask what something costs and why.** The price that vendor just quoted you might give you sticker shock, but there's likely a very good reason they charge what they charge. Ask. If you're getting priced out from a vendor you must have for your wedding, consider other items you can reduce or cut from your budget.

2. **Don't ghost.** Yes, it's awkward to tell someone that you're not going to hire them, but it's much more respectful than leaving them hanging. A simple one-sentence email can do wonders, and as a bonus, it respects the vendor. They now know for certain if they can book another wedding on that date.

3. **Don't over-rotate.** Researching vendors can quickly turn into a part-time job. Set yourself a goal of a vendor a month and be rigorous about how many options you research and interview. Whenever possible, share the load with your partner.

4. **Don't micromanage.** Sometimes when we're stressed, we hold on tighter when it would be best to let go. Check that impulse. Trust that you've hired quality people who know what they're doing (and have been to a lot more weddings than you have).

5. **Don't support people who don't celebrate everyone's joy.** Do Black lives matter to the vendor you're thinking of hiring? Are LGBTQIA+ couples safe with them? Are people of color? Hire vendors who make it clear whose joy matters to them.

PHOTOS AND VIDEO

For some couples, the images of their wedding day are of utmost importance. Others want one nice photo to hang on the wall. Identify where you and your partner fall on this continuum. Budget accordingly. Photography is often more expensive than might be expected because of the amount of labor that goes into editing.

The same advice holds true for videography. Time and again, a wedding video is the one memento that couples tell me they treasure the most. That doesn't mean it's the right fit for everyone. I knew this advice, and my husband and I didn't opt for a videographer, because neither of us is the type of person who would make a point to watch a video on our anniversary. Talk through the idea with your partner rather than discount it right from the start.

Whatever your final choices on photos and video, recognize that you have options. There's a huge variety of wedding photographers and videographers. Many have taken the craft and elevated it to an art form that incorporates documentary and photojournalism techniques.

If you and your partner prioritize art and design in your life as a couple, explore what that looks like when it comes to wedding day imagery. If you don't care all that much about art and design, own that and spend your money on services you identify with more. Give yourself the freedom to say no so you can afford to say yes where it matters to you.

PHOTO AND VIDEO: MUST-ASK QUESTIONS

1. **How many hours are we hiring you for?** Often, you hire a photographer and/or videographer for a set number of hours. Those hours may end before your reception does. That's not usually a big deal unless there's something you particularly want them to capture at the end of the day. In that case, ask what an extra hour or two would cost.

2. **When will you start?** You won't usually get an answer to this question during the interview; it'll come later when we create your timeline in chapter 12 (page 175). For now, make a note to regroup closer to the wedding.

3. **Are you familiar with the wedding location(s)?** This is not a deal breaker, just a nice-to-have. Usually a photographer or videographer will arrive a little early on the wedding day to scout a location they're not familiar with.

4. **Will you be hiring a second shooter?** Again, not a deal breaker. Just a good question to ask so you can know who's on your team and if you need to feed them.

5. **LGBTQIA+ couples, ask if they pose straight couples and LGBTQIA+ couples the same way.** The answer should be no since the same old wedding poses are often heteronormative.

6. **How do you make your couples feel comfortable?** This is a good way to see if they'll vibe with you so you can relax enough to enjoy having your photo taken.

7. **How are you at cat-herding?** A vital skill for handling VIPs.

8. **Is an engagement shoot required?** Often photographers use engagement shoots to establish rapport, so they may offer this at a discount.

9. **How much will this service cost?** Remember that the fee includes the labor of editing.

10. **When can we expect the final product?** Usually this is at least six weeks after the wedding. Plan accordingly.

COMPARING PHOTOGRAPHERS AND VIDEOGRAPHERS

	NAME(S) AND PRONOUNS	CONTACT INFORMATION	AVAILABLE? (Y/N)	HOURS	WHAT ARE THEY SELLING US?
PHOTO-GRAPHER 1					
PHOTO-GRAPHER 2					
PHOTO-GRAPHER 3					
VIDEO-GRAPHER 1					
VIDEO-GRAPHER 2					
VIDEO-GRAPHER 3					

CONSIDER THIS

When considering a service that is less important to you than other services, research "elopement" options. This is wedding industry jargon for a smaller scale of service such as two to four hours of coverage versus six to ten hours.

WILL WE BE FEEDING THEM? (Y/N)	FEE	EXPERIENCE	STYLE/TONE	TOP THREE PROS	TOP THREE CONS	OVERALL RATING (1 TO 5)

SELECTING A PHOTOGRAPHER AND/OR VIDEOGRAPHER

Photography

This is how we're capturing photos on our wedding day:

_____

_____

This is what this service costs:

_____

_____

If someone is handling this service for us, that person's name and contact information are:

_____

_____

_____

_____

These are other details that we want to remember. (Examples include payment deadlines and if/when you owe final timings and a shot list to the vendor in question.)

_____

_____

_____

_____

Videography

This is how we're capturing video on our wedding day:

_____

_____

_____

This is what this service costs:

_____

_____

_____

_____

If someone is handling this service for us, that person's name and contact information are:

_____

_____

_____

_____

These are other details that we want to remember. (Examples include payment deadlines, any equipment you and your partner are responsible for arranging, and if/when you owe final timings and a shot list to the vendor in question.)

_____

_____

_____

_____

CREATING A SHOT LIST

Not all of the examples below will apply to your situation. Instead, consider this as a template to fit to your purposes.

If you two have people who are accompanying you during the ceremony:

THE COUPLE WITH:
- Partner 1's party
- Individual members of Partner 1's party
- Partner 2's party
- Individual members of Partner 2's party
- Officiant(s)

PARTNER 1 WITH:

- Partner 1's party
- Individual members of Partner 1's party
- Partner 2's party
- Individual members of Partner 2's party
- Officiant(s)

PARTNER 2 WITH:

- Partner 1's party
- Individual members of Partner 1's party
- Partner 2's party
- Individual members of Partner 2's party
- Officiant(s)

If you two have families—biological and/or chosen—attending the wedding:

PARTNER 1'S SIDE OF THE FAMILY

THE COUPLE WITH:

- Partner 1's immediate family
- Partner 1's parent(s) or guardian(s)—individual (e.g., a photo per parent or guardian) and together
- Partner 1's sibling(s)—individual and together
- Partner 1's maternal grandparents(s)
- Partner 1's maternal aunt(s), uncle(s), and/or cousin(s)
- Partner 1's maternal relatives (additional)
- Partner 1's paternal grandparent(s)
- Partner 1's paternal aunt(s), uncle(s), and/or cousin(s)
- Partner 1's paternal relatives (additional)
- Partner 1's chosen family (additional)

PARTNER 1 WITH:

- Partner 1's immediate family
- Partner 1's parent(s) or guardian(s)—individual (e.g., a photo per parent or guardian) and together
- Partner 1's sibling(s)—individual and together
- Partner 1's maternal grandparents(s)
- Partner 1's maternal aunt(s), uncle(s), and/or cousin(s)

- Partner 1's maternal relatives (additional)
- Partner 1's paternal grandparent(s)
- Partner 1's paternal aunt(s), uncle(s), and/or cousin(s)
- Partner 1's paternal relatives (additional)
- Partner 1's chosen family (additional)

PARTNER 2 WITH:

- Partner 1's immediate family
- Partner 1's parent(s) or guardian(s)—individual (e.g., a photo per parent or guardian) and together
- Partner 1's sibling(s)—individual and together
- Partner 1's maternal grandparents(s)
- Partner 1's maternal aunt(s), uncle(s), and/or cousin(s)
- Partner 1's maternal relatives (additional)
- Partner 1's paternal grandparent(s)
- Partner 1's paternal aunt(s), uncle(s), and/or cousin(s)
- Partner 1's paternal relatives (additional)
- Partner 1's chosen family (additional)

PARTNER 2'S SIDE OF THE FAMILY

THE COUPLE WITH:

- Partner 2's immediate family
- Partner 2's parent(s) or guardian(s)—individual (e.g., a photo per parent or guardian) and together
- Partner 2's sibling(s)—individual and together
- Partner 2's maternal grandparents(s)
- Partner 2's maternal aunt(s), uncle(s), and/or cousin(s)
- Partner 2's maternal relatives (additional)
- Partner 2's paternal grandparent(s)
- Partner 2's paternal aunt(s), uncle(s), and/or cousin(s)
- Partner 2's paternal relatives (additional)
- Partner 2's chosen family (additional)

PARTNER 2 WITH:

- Partner 2's immediate family
- Partner 2's parent(s) or guardian(s)—individual (e.g., a photo per parent or guardian) and together
- Partner 2's sibling(s)—individual and together

- Partner 2's maternal grandparents(s)
- Partner 2's maternal aunt(s), uncle(s), and/or cousin(s)
- Partner 2's maternal relatives (additional)
- Partner 2's paternal grandparent(s)
- Partner 2's paternal aunt(s), uncle(s), and/or cousin(s)
- Partner 2's paternal relatives (additional)
- Partner 2's chosen family (additional)

PARTNER 1 WITH:

- Partner 2's immediate family
- Partner 2's parent(s) or guardian(s)—individual (e.g., a photo per parent or guardian) and together
- Partner 2's sibling(s)—individual and together
- Partner 2's maternal grandparents(s)
- Partner 2's maternal aunt(s), uncle(s), and/or cousin(s)
- Partner 2's maternal relatives (additional)
- Partner 2's paternal grandparent(s)
- Partner 2's paternal aunt(s), uncle(s), and/or cousin(s)
- Partner 2's paternal relatives (additional)
- Partner 2's chosen family (additional)

More Shots

Are there any groups of people who may not qualify as chosen or biological family but whom you still want a photo with? Examples: Partner 2's former roommates, Partner 1's softball team, etc.

_____

_____

_____

Are there any particular moments at the wedding that you want to make sure to capture? Examples: when one partner sees the other partner walking down the aisle, a VIP's toast, etc.

_____

_____

_____

Are there any details of the wedding day that you want to make sure to capture? Examples: close-up photos of rings and/or certain items of clothing, decorations, food, etc.

MUSIC

As you consider what to play at your wedding, think about what music brings you and your partner joy. What was the first concert you attended as a couple? Is there a song that holds special significance in your relationship? Would it be meaningful to have a certain guest perform?

The answers to these questions may not be what you think of when you think of "wedding music." That's okay. Take the opportunity of planning your wedding to harness the power of music. You're trying to create certain feelings that you and your partner identified as important to experience when your marriage begins (the ceremony) and when your loved ones celebrate (the reception).

While considering music, also discuss who will be the wedding's MC. This is an important role because, depending on the wedding's size and activities, you'll need someone to cue people to eat, toast, and/or dance. Often, the MC role is filled by a DJ or bandleader, but it can be filled by a guest. (I find it's usually one who has a background in theater.) Talk through what this looks like and consider writing a script for anyone who doesn't regularly work weddings.

MUSIC: MUST-ASK QUESTIONS

1. **How many hours are we hiring you for?** Consider if those hours cover the activities you need this person to provide music for, such as a ceremony, cocktail hour, and/or reception.

2. **Do you have any specific setup needs?** This typically means access to outlets and a large enough space to set up the music or DJ booth.

3. **Will you need any tech provided?** Think: a microphone on a stand, a free-standing mic and/or lapel mic(s), and Wi-Fi.

4. **When will you need our final song selections?** This is most applicable if you're hiring a DJ. Often, the vendor will provide a worksheet for you and your partner to fill out closer to your wedding day.

5. **Will we need amplified sound?** In nearly all situations, the answer is yes. This is particularly true if you're hosting any part of your wedding outdoors. Talk through solutions so your guests can actually hear what you're saying.

6. **How much will this service cost?** Remember that the fee includes the labor of setup and/or potentially equipment rental.

7. **Are you comfortable playing MC at our wedding?** It's useful if you can provide examples of what you mean by this, such as "We will need someone to cue a buffet line" or "We are expecting a few toasts. How do you assist with that?"

CEREMONY MUSIC

For Part 1, assign one to two adjectives to each of the places in a wedding where music often appears. These adjectives should describe the feeling that you two want your guests and yourselves to experience at these times.

Part 1

OUR CEREMONY

Entering (Often, this is one or two songs. For example, a couple may enter the ceremony together and opt for one song. Another couple may have one song play as Partner 1 and any VIPs enter and then a second song when Partner 2 enters.)

Leaving (Often, one song.)

_____

Before our main meal (For example, during a happy hour.)

_____

_____

After our main meal (If you and your partner are planning to do any first dances such as a dance together or a dance with certain VIPs, these often happen after the wedding's main meal. You don't have to dance for the whole song.)

_____

_____

After any first dances (This is what people often think of as "the dance party," if applicable.)

_____

_____

Part 2

After you've assigned adjectives, brainstorm certain artists, songs, or genres of music that evoke those feelings in you and your partner. Use that information to guide your song selection(s).

_____

_____

_____

BUILDING A PLAYLIST

Outline your final music selections. Be specific about song title, artist, and, as applicable, version. Also include any edits that you may want to certain songs (e.g., "Cut the song at minute 2:32" or "Fade out at minute 1:45").

During our ceremony, we will play:

Before our main meal, we will play:

If we're having dessert and want to play a specific song at that time, we will play:

If we are having first dances, we will play:

These are certain group dances that we want to include at our wedding:

These are artists, songs, or genres of music that we do want played at our wedding:

These are artists, songs, or genres of music that we do not want played at our wedding:

....

....

This is what music will cost at our wedding:

....

....

WRITING A SCRIPT FOR AN MC

If you're arranging an MC for your wedding, use this template to write a script they can follow. This exercise likely won't be necessary if you're hiring a professional DJ or band.

- [time] .... — Couple enters reception
- *MC says*: "I'd like to welcome [specify how you'd like to be introduced]."
- *Tip*: If your MC or DJ doesn't know how to pronounce your names, offer a pronunciation guide (e.g., "e-liz-a-beth kra-mer").

- [time] .... — Meal service begins (if buffet)
- *MC says*: "[insert meal, typically dinner] is now available. [Insert details on how tables will be dismissed, if people can grab food at will, etc.]"

- [time] .... — Toasts start
- *MC says*: "I'd like to invite [insert relationship to the couple], [insert name of person presenting toast, and, as needed, pronunciation of their name], to the mic."

- [time] .... — First bite
- *MC says*: "I'd like to invite all of our guests to [insert location] for the couple's first bite."

- [time] .... — First dance(s)
- **SONG**: [specify song title and artist]

- *MC says*: "I'd like to invite the couple out on the dance floor for their first dance."
- **SONG**: [specify song title and artist]
- *MC says*: "I'd like to invite [the specific partner and their VIP of choice] out on the dance floor."

- [time] _____ — Bouquet and/or garter toss
- *MC says*: "It's time for the [insert partner's or partners' name(s)] to toss the [bouquet or garter]! All who'd like to participate, please gather at the center of the dance floor."

- [time] _____ — Last call
- *MC says*: "Heads-up: The bar's about to close, so grab any last drinks!"

- [time] _____ — Couple's departure
- *MC says*: "I'd like to invite all of our guests to [insert location] to wish the couple on their way! [Add any specifics if your guests should pick up a sparkler, bubbles, etc., for the exit.]"

CONSIDER THIS

If you're providing your own music, assign someone to the device that will be used. Give them three tips: First, download the playlist to the device before leaving regular Wi-Fi. Second, for anything Bluetooth, be sure to reconnect if you walk away. Third, instead of abruptly cutting off the music, gradually lower the volume so it fades out.

FOOD AND DRINK

What you feed your guests is one of the easiest ways to inspire a particular feeling at your wedding. It can also be a special opportunity to showcase cuisines, dishes, or ingredients that have certain meanings to you and your partner.

While picking your menu, keep a few etiquette tips in mind. First, not everyone can eat everything. Ask your guests for food allergies, restrictions, or preferences. Then relay that information to the people responsible for the food. The same goes for alcohol. Not everyone drinks, so be sure to provide nonalcoholic options, too.

Second, err on the side of too much rather than too little. This can get expensive, so when in doubt, opt for cheap and plenty rather than expensive and not enough. Hungry guests are not happy guests.

Third, get creative when it comes to catering. Brunch, exclusively dessert, food carts, pizza—all are worthy options when it comes to feeding people en masse. The trick is to set expectations. If you're not planning to provide a full dinner, tell your guests so they can plan accordingly.

FOOD AND DRINK: MUST-ASK QUESTIONS

1. **Are you familiar with the wedding location(s)?** It's not a deal breaker if they're not. Rather, use this question to discuss what the caterer needs to do their job, such as on-site ovens, prep areas, elevators, etc.

2. **Who's handling the rentals?** "Rentals" here means plates and utensils (for all meal services), glasses (including any specialty glasses like for a champagne toast or custom cocktail), and linens (napkins plus tablecloths for guest tables and non-guest tables like a DJ booth or gift table).

3. **Will we have a tasting? If so, when and how many people can we invite? What will the tasting cost?**

4. **How large will your team be and why?** The factor that often influences this answer is whether the main meal is plated (bigger staff because of tableside service) or buffet (smaller staff). This matters because more people will cost more money, but do trust what your caterer tells you. They know their team best.

5. **How do you handle food allergies, restrictions, and preferences?** This is particularly important when discussing severe allergies or dietary requirements like halal or kosher.

6. **Who will handle the bar? Is the bar team licensed?** Depending on your venue, you may also need to provide liquor liability insurance yourselves.

7. **How much alcohol and nonalcohol will we need?** You can also google "drink calculator" yourselves.

8. **When will you need our final menu and/or drink selections?** Be sure to communicate if you're independently sourcing a particular food or drink. For example, "We're buying a cake from this baker" or "We'll be providing all of the wine from Costco."

9. **Who's doing the dishes?** This is particularly important if you're also arranging the rentals.

10. **What do you do with the leftovers?** There's a chance you'll be responsible for taking them home and perhaps even providing the to-go boxes.

11. **Where does the trash, recycling, and compost go after the wedding?** Often, but not always, this is somewhere on-site at the venue.

12. **How much will this service cost?** Remember that the fee likely includes a tip, but may not include rentals and/or alcohol.

COMPARING CATERING OPTIONS

	NAME(S) AND PRONOUNS	CONTACT INFORMATION	AVAILABLE FOR OUR WEDDING? (Y/N)	WHAT MEAL AND/ OR BEVERAGE SERVICE(S) ARE WE HIRING THEM FOR?
CATERING OPTION 1				
CATERING OPTION 2				
CATERING OPTION 3				

CHOOSING THE FOOD

Outline your final selections for all things food at your wedding. Don't include dessert; we'll cover this later.

These are the meals we're arranging for our wedding (e.g., a main meal, a happy hour, a "late-night snack" for later in the reception, etc.):

....

....

....

....

....

ARE THEY HANDLING THE RENT-ALS? IF SO, WHICH RENTALS?	ARE THEY DOING THE DISHES? (Y/N)	ARE WE DOING A TASTING? IF SO, WHEN AND WHAT DOES IT COST?	FEE (INCLUD-ING ANY TRAVEL AND/OR STAFFING COSTS)	TOP THREE PROS	TOP THREE CONS	OVERALL RATING (1 TO 5)

These are the people or places providing each meal:

_____

_____

_____

_____

This is what each service listed above costs:

_____

_____

_____

_____

These are the meals we're arranging ourselves (e.g., breakfast/lunch/snacks before the wedding):

_____

_____

_____

_____

This is what each meal we're arranging ourselves will cost:

These are other details we want to remember. (Examples include allergies and preferences, rentals to arrange, tastings to attend, etc.)

CONSIDER THIS

Don't get hung up on whether you're hosting a full bar. People don't think this is rude as long as you're clear about what is and isn't covered. A nice middle option: Tell the bar staff to move to a cash bar when your tab hits a certain amount.

CHOOSING THE DRINKS

Use this worksheet to record what drinks you and your partner plan to offer.

Before our ceremony, these are the drinks we'll offer (e.g., water for an outdoor summer wedding, pre-ceremony bar, etc.):

After our ceremony, these are the alcoholic drinks we'll offer (e.g., full bar, cash bar, wine only, wine/beer only, etc.):

After our ceremony, these are the nonalcoholic drinks we'll offer (e.g., water, coffee [decaf and/or regular], tea, sodas, lemonade, mocktails, juice, sparkling cider, etc.):

_____

_____

_____

_____

_____

If we're having any special drinks, we'll offer these (e.g., cocktails, hot cocoa bar, custom cocktail, champagne or other specialty drink toast):

_____

_____

_____

_____

This is what drinks will cost at our wedding. (Include what they will cost you and what they will cost your guests, as applicable.)

_____

_____

_____

_____

_____

_____

These are other details we want to remember. (Examples include anything you might be sourcing, such as a tap, ice, and/or garnishes, as well as who's responsible for serving which drinks.)

....

....

....

....

CONSIDER THIS

Certain beverages require more work than others. For example, if you're offering beer out of a keg, be very clear about who is tapping the keg, when they're doing it, and with what equipment as provided by which people. Nothing holds up the bar line faster than a finicky keg.

DESSERT

When we think of "wedding dessert," cake may come to mind. But just like with the rest of your menu, tie any dessert to your relationship for the most meaningful—and delicious—result.

Also, talk to your partner about if you two want what's often called a "first bite." As with all "firsts" at a wedding, the term denotes the first time two people do something as a married couple. In this case, we mean the first time two people feed each other a bite of food. My only advice here? If you do this, please first ask your partner before rubbing food all over their face.

Dessert at a wedding may also involve certain implements, such as a family heirloom or champagne saber. Keep this in mind as you plan. Don't hesitate to go smaller on one dessert you don't really want to eat (such as a cake to cut with great-grandpa's military sword) so you can go larger on something you do want to eat (like that custom macaron tower you've been eyeing).

DESSERT: MUST-ASK QUESTIONS

1. **Will we have a tasting? If so, when and for how many? What will it cost?**

2. **How do you handle food allergies, restrictions, and preferences?** This is particularly important when discussing severe allergies or dietary requirements like halal or kosher.

3. **Will we want delivery or pickup?** If the latter, make a note to assign someone to handle the pickup on the actual wedding day.

4. **When will you need our final selections?** This likely means providing a specific order number and/or flavor(s).

5. **Is there anything we need to provide you and, if so, by when?** (e.g., a cake topper, decorative flowers, etc.)

6. **Do you provide any equipment, or should we source our own?** Think cake stands, cupcake stands, doughnut wall, etc. If you get it from the dessert-maker, remember to return it.

7. **What should we do with the leftovers?** Some people opt to freeze their wedding dessert to eat again on an anniversary. If that's your thing, make sure your chosen dessert will hold up.

8. **If you're arranging for a loved one to make dessert, what help will they need?** "Help" means arranging people to frost cupcakes, move desserts to and from different locations, sourcing ingredients, etc.

9. **How much will this service cost?** Factor in delivery, pickup, and/or any ingredients you may be providing.

CONSIDER THIS

Make sure signage is available for what's in certain foods, particularly for food allergies, restrictions, and preferences. How you share this information can range from a menu to small signs next to the food itself. Discuss options with whomever is providing the food.

COMPARING DESSERTS

	NAME(S) AND PRONOUNS	CONTACT INFORMATION	AVAILABLE FOR OUR WEDDING? (Y/N)	WHAT ARE THEY MAKING US?	HOW MUCH ARE THEY MAKING?
DESSERT OPTION 1					
DESSERT OPTION 2					
DESSERT OPTION 3					

CONSIDER THIS

Expect to feed any vendor who is working your wedding when food is served. Often, this is three to five people and will likely not include any catering team (they'll feed themselves). Vendor plates are often discounted, but check to make sure they're actually edible meals and not a bunch of sad sandwiches in brown paper bags.

IS THERE ANYTHING WE NEED TO PROVIDE FOR THEM?	DELIVERY OR PICKUP?	ARE WE DOING A TASTING? IF SO, WHEN AND WHAT DOES IT COST?	FEE (INCLUDING ANY TRAVEL AND/OR RENTALS)	TOP THREE PROS	TOP THREE CONS	OVERALL RATING (1 TO 5)

OUR FINAL MENU

Before our ceremony, this is the food we'll offer (usually not applicable):

_____

_____

Immediately after our ceremony, this is the food we'll offer (e.g., appetizers, cheese plates, not applicable if you move right into a main meal, etc.):

_____

_____

This is the main meal we'll offer (include all elements and remember that "main meal" can mean something like "potluck," with each dish assigned to a guest, or "dessert buffet"):

If we're providing dessert, it will be:

If we're providing any additional food, it will be (e.g., food specific for kids, a late-night snack, vegan candy for a vegan candy bar, etc.):

This is what food will cost at our wedding:

These are other details that we want to remember:

9

Decor, Rentals, Flowers, and More

How your wedding looks is often a top concern—perhaps not for you and your partner but for people who care about you. If you haven't already, plan to regularly start fielding questions that include the words "style," "vibe," and our old frenemy "vision."

In terms of etiquette, consider why people are suddenly so concerned about decor. Usually, it's because the topic is low-hanging conversational fruit. It's much easier to talk about color palettes than the deep inner work you and your partner are doing as you contemplate this big thing called "marriage."

Hold space for this reality. Challenge yourselves not to resort to the (understandable) knee-jerk reaction of an eye roll when the millionth person asks, "What are your colors?" Even better, consider who in your life has a certain talent that might shine at your wedding. Invite them in.

As you do, keep talking to your partner. Work together to figure out how the aesthetics of your wedding can contribute to your overall mission statement. Different flowers, colors, and gifts evoke different feelings. Harness this to move your wedding closer to that mission statement you two set way back in chapter 1 (page 7).

You can make this process of decorating as complicated and involved as you two desire. No matter what, please remember one thing: The fate of your marriage does not hinge on table linens. Keep this in mind and you'll be surprised at how fun wedding decor can suddenly become.

COUPLE 1

The night before her wedding, Lindsay informed her bridesmaids that they would be spending the evening making their own bouquets. None of them had ever done this before. The result was a stressful, tear-filled evening that left everyone ragged and resentful.

COUPLE 2

When contemplating how they wanted to thank their guests, Daryl and Christopher considered what people could actually use at their wedding. They wanted a wedding favor that wouldn't immediately end up in a landfill. The result: small jars of jam to use during dinner.

TOP FIVE ETIQUETTE DOS

1. **Do set expectations.** It's not rude to ask a guest to perform a certain function at your wedding as long as you set very clear, very honest expectations about what, when, and how they're doing that function. Help them help you.

2. **Do prioritize sustainability.** The average wedding produces somewhere in the neighborhood of 400 pounds of garbage and 63 tons of carbon dioxide. Use tools like the *Less Stuff, More Meaning Wedding Footprint Calculator* to offset the damage (see the Additional Resources on page 195). Hire vendors whose work is sustainable. Recycle. Reuse.

3. **Do consider secondhand.** It saves you money, and it saves the planet. Scout options online. Then, when you're done, consider paying it forward to another couple.

4. **Do remember any flowers.** The easiest—though more expensive—way is to hire your florist to return at the end of the party. Depending on how the flowers were grown and their own business practices, the florist will reuse the raw materials and compost the rest. If that's not an option, research ways to donate wedding flowers. Certain wedding vendors and third-party businesses offer this service; hospitals or retirement homes may also welcome such donations.

5. **Do pick your battles.** Is your soon-to-be mother-in-law insisting that she make you decorations that you don't actually want? Rather than fight about it, evaluate her motivation. Is this an affordable way she can share in your joy? Does it detract from yours? If it doesn't, let her craft. If it does, re-establish boundaries and perhaps find another way she can contribute.

TOP FIVE ETIQUETTE DON'TS

1. **Don't jerk your vendors around.** Nothing undermines a vendor more than last-minute messages that radically change a finalized order. This is particularly true for items like food or flowers that require the vendor to order materials well in advance. When you make your final choice, stick with it. Respect the time and talent of your team.

2. **Don't get angry when your guests forget their favors.** This is an honest mistake, usually caused by one too many drinks. The same goes for flowers: Your inebriated guests may not want your centerpieces.

3. **Don't say no to every offer of help.** Guests mean it when they ask, "How can I help?" They love you, and helping might also be an economical way for them to contribute to your wedding. Ask what they're thinking and see if it aligns with your mission.

4. **Don't forget that all of this has to be cleaned up.** Often, the people doing the cleaning are the very guests you don't want to lift a finger. Is there someone you can hire to handle these tasks? If that's not an option, how can you minimize what needs to be boxed up at the end of the event?

5. **Don't forget to say thank you.** When it comes to decor and rentals, you're likely hiring people you will never meet to do physical labor you will never see. Be gracious, and, when possible, tip. Writing an online review also makes a big difference and can be a nice way to say thanks if a tip isn't possible.

CONSIDER THIS

As soon as you monogram something, its resale value plummets. This doesn't mean don't do it; just be aware of what you do and don't customize.

EVENT DECOR AND SETUP

To figure out your event decor and setup, start from a place of "How much stuff do we want?" This is important because it's very easy to decorate your wedding on autopilot. That's how you suddenly end up with 18 overflowing cardboard boxes lining the hallway of your apartment. Instead, be specific about what you want and why you want it. Prioritize decor that serves a purpose ("to be pretty" totally counts).

Next, delegate. Consider who's already on your team (i.e., your vendors) and ask polite but specific questions about who does what. For example, a caterer will often have no problem setting out place cards as long as they're given enough notice and provided clear instructions. A florist will usually set up any centerpieces or other floral decorations for a small fee.

The people doing these tasks don't have to be professionals. Of course, it helps if they are, but anyone who tells you it's a requirement is probably selling you something. Rather than throw money you don't have at the problem, consider what the problem actually is. Are there people who aren't coming to the wedding—such as the eager teen children of a friendly coworker—who could help out? Get creative. Whenever possible, pay these people, at least a little, and consider thanking them with a note, reference, or other small token of gratitude.

DECOR INSPIRATION

Wedding decor is often thought of as "a girl thing." That's problematic for a lot of reasons, so please uninvite gender norms as you fill out this worksheet together. As needed, refer to the "Our Ideal Ceremony" and "Our Ideal Reception" worksheets in chapter 4 (pages 42 and 45).

Ceremony Decor

1. How do we want our guests to feel during our ceremony? How do we want to feel during our ceremony?

_____

_____

_____

_____

2. If we weren't talking about a wedding, what are ways that we would evoke those types of feelings?

_____

_____

_____

_____

3. How could the answer to Question 2 be adapted to decor at our wedding ceremony?

_____

_____

_____

_____

Reception Decor

1. How do we want our guests to feel during our reception? How do we want to feel during our reception?

    ....

    ....

    ....

    ....

2. If we weren't talking about a wedding, what are ways that we would evoke those types of feelings?

    ....

    ....

    ....

    ....

3. How could the answer to Question 2 be adapted to decor at our wedding reception?

    ....

    ....

    ....

    ....

CHOOSING YOUR RENTALS

Most items on the list aren't required, and a vendor may handle some of them, depending on the situation. Check off those you want and need.

Ceremony

- ☐ Someplace for your guests to sit (It's okay to ask people to stand as long as you make accommodations for those who cannot stand for long periods of time and/or may have small children to attend to.)
- ☐ Chair covers and/or cushions (if you're having chairs)
- ☐ A/V (Think: mics, mic stands, amps, speakers, and, depending on the setting, a generator)

- ☐ Table(s) (Think: any table you want to greet guests where you might display ceremony-specific information like a program.)
- ☐ Any ceremony-specific decorations you want to rent
- ☐ Any custom lighting you want
- ☐ Tent(s)
- ☐ Restrooms
- ☐ Blankets (depending on when and where the ceremony is happening)

Reception

- ☐ Anything your guests will need in order to eat (e.g., plates and utensils—enough sets for every meal service)
- ☐ Anything your guests will need in order to drink (e.g., specific

barware and glasses—enough for every type of beverage)
- ☐ Anything you need for beverages (e.g., keg-tapping materials, etc.)

- [ ] Someplace for your guests to sit (It's okay if these are the same seats used for the ceremony. Just be clear about who's moving the chairs from point A to point B. "The guests" is a perfectly acceptable answer. Ask that the officiant(s) cue them to do so.)
- [ ] Chair covers and/or cushions (if you're having chairs)
- [ ] A/V (Think: mics, mic stands, amps, speakers and, depending on the setting, a generator)
- [ ] Tables (both for sitting and eating at, and to display various reception-specific items like a guest book, gifts, favors, dessert, beverages, etc.)
- [ ] Linens (napkins and/or table-cloths for *all* tables)
- [ ] Lawn games, board games, puzzles, etc.

COMPARING RENTAL COMPANIES

	NAME(S) AND PRONOUNS	CONTACT INFORMATION	AVAILABLE FOR OUR WEDDING? (Y/N)	WHAT ARE WE RENTING FROM THEM?
RENTAL COMPANY 1				
RENTAL COMPANY 2				
RENTAL COMPANY 3				

- [ ] Items for a photo booth (e.g., backdrop, stand for a camera or iPad, etc.)
- [ ] Anything for kids (often high-chairs, but perhaps toys, too)
- [ ] Any reception-specific decorations you want to rent
- [ ] Any custom lighting you want
- [ ] Tent(s)
- [ ] Dance floor
- [ ] Lounge furniture (Some couples want to create certain "hangout areas" for their guests. If that's you, then you might rent furniture for this.)
- [ ] Restrooms

HOW ARE WE GETTING THE ITEM(S)?	WHO IS SETTING UP THESE ITEMS?	HOW ARE WE RETURNING THE ITEM(S)? AND WHERE THE ITEM(S) ARE DUE	FEE	TOP THREE PROS	TOP THREE CONS	OVERALL RATING (1 TO 5)

FINAL RENTAL SELECTIONS AND DETAILS

Ceremony

These are the rentals we need:

....

....

....

....

This is who is providing these rentals (include contact information plus when and where the rentals will arrive):

....

....

....

....

This is who is setting up these rentals before our ceremony begins (include contact information):

....

....

....

....

This is what the rentals will cost:

....

....

These are other details we want to remember:

....

....

Reception

These are the rentals we need:

....

....

....

This is who is providing these rentals (include contact information plus when and where the rentals will arrive):

....

....

....

This is who is setting up these rentals before our reception begins (include contact information):

....

....

....

....

This is what the rentals will cost:

....

....

These are other details we want to remember:

....

....

....

After the Wedding

These are the rentals that need to be returned after the wedding (include when
and where the rentals need to be returned):

....

....

....

....

This is who is returning these rentals before they are due back (include contact
information):

....

....

....

....

These are other details we want to remember:

....

....

FLOWERS AND FAVORS

Flowers and favors present two wonderful opportunities to let artistry into your wedding. They're also a common cause of sticker shock. Thankfully, because of the heavy lifting you did back in chapter 2 (page 17), we know where both items fall on our priority list.

As you and your partner begin to brainstorm, I encourage you to work in tandem with whoever may be providing these items. A florist, for example, will have a deep knowledge of flowers that, if you let them share it with you, can elevate your wedding flowers from a place of "just something I saw on Pinterest" to "custom art installation that enhances our entire wedding day."

The same is true for favors. Consider what local stores or artisans you and your partner like whom you might be able to support. Challenge yourselves to think of a favor that plays an active part in your wedding, rather than something guests will only throw away. Think of a wedding favor as the cherry on the sundae: completely not necessary but a delicious final touch.

FLOWERS: MUST-ASK QUESTIONS

1. **How are the flowers grown?** We're looking for words like "organic," "sustainable," "micro-flower farming," and "in-season."

2. **Where are the flowers being sourced?** Any real flowers that are flown in have a much higher carbon footprint than local flowers do. If you're considering fake flowers, how were they made?

3. *If you're talking to a florist or doing your own flowers:* **Do you use flower foam?** The best—and, some would argue, only—answer is no since there are many more sustainable ways to construct flower arrangements, including chicken wire, kenzan (a spiky device to keep flowers in place), and water tubes.

4. **How do the flowers get to the wedding?** If the answer is a pickup, make a note to assign someone this task so you get your flowers before the ceremony or any pre-ceremony photos begin.

5. **Do the vases come with the order? If so, do we need to return them and by when?**

6. *If you're talking to a florist:* **What is one creative idea you have for our wedding?**

7. *If you're talking to a florist:* **Do you offer à la carte options?** Ask this question if flowers are lower down on your priorities list, as this option can allow you to buy a smaller overall order.

8. *If you're talking to a florist:* **Can you return at the end of the wedding? If so, is this an additional cost? If not, any recommendations on how we dispose of the flowers?**

9. **How much will this service cost?**

FLOWER INSPIRATION

Wedding flowers come in two categories: personals and decorative. "Personals" refer to any flowers a person wears or carries, such as bouquets, boutonnieres, corsages, and flower crowns. "Decorative" refers to any flowers used to decorate the ceremony and/or reception, such as centerpieces, flower arches, and flowers for the cake. Use these definitions as you and your partner brainstorm if/how you want to incorporate flowers on your wedding day.

Ceremony Flowers

1. What adjectives and feelings have we previously used in this book to describe our ceremony?

....

....

2. When we think of our ceremony, do any particular colors, scents, shapes, and/or flower types come to mind? (It's okay if the answer here is no.)

....

....

3. Whom do we want to carry or wear flowers during our ceremony (i.e., your personals)? Be careful to not assume gender as you make these choices, as certain floral arrangements have certain gendered connotations (i.e., "girls carry bouquets and boys wear boutonnieres"). When in doubt, ask your VIPs what they would prefer.

4. Where do we want to display flowers during our ceremony (i.e., your decorative flowers)?

Reception Flowers

1. What adjectives and feelings have we previously used in this book to describe our reception?

2. When we think of our reception, do any particular colors, scents, shapes, and/or flower types come to mind? (It's okay if the answer here is no.)

3. Whom do we want to carry or wear flowers during our reception (i.e., your personals)?

....

....

....

....

4. Where do we want to display flowers during our reception (i.e., your decorative flowers)?

....

....

....

....

CONSIDER THIS

Flowers can make lovely thank-you gifts for The Board and other VIPs. A corsage, boutonniere, or other personal flower arrangement tells guests and vendors, "Hey, here's someone important who helped with our wedding."

MAKING FLOWER SELECTIONS

Ceremony

These are our flowers for our ceremony:

_____

_____

_____

_____

This is who is providing these flowers (include contact information and when and where the flowers will arrive):

_____

_____

This is who is setting up these flowers before our ceremony begins (include contact information):

_____

_____

This is what the flowers will cost:

_____

_____

These are other details that we want to remember:

_____

_____

Reception

These are our flowers for our reception:

_____

_____

_____

_____

This is who is providing these flowers (include contact information and when and where the flowers will arrive):

_____

_____

This is who is setting up these flowers before our reception begins (include contact information):

_____

_____

This is what the flowers will cost:

_____

_____

These are other details that we want to remember:

_____

_____

After the Wedding

This is what we're doing with the flowers after our wedding:

These are the flower-related items that need to be returned after our wedding (include when and where the items need to be returned):

This is who is returning these items before the items are due back (include contact information):

These are other details that we want to remember:

CHOOSING FAVORS

Use this worksheet to brainstorm what kind of favors you two may or may not want for your wedding. Favors are not required and can come in many forms, including photos from a photo booth or a certain food to eat alongside a main meal.

1. How do we want our guests to feel when they leave our wedding?

    ....

    ....

    ....

    ....

2. If we weren't talking about a wedding, what are ways that we would evoke those types of feelings?

    ....

    ....

    ....

3. How could the answer to Question 2 be adapted to favors?

    ....

    ....

    ....

4. Do we want our favors to serve a function at our wedding? (For instance, do we want the favors to serve as place cards, too?)

_____

_____

5. Do our favors cause any damage to the environment? (For example, are these seeds native to the area where our guests will plant them? How much waste do these favors produce?)

_____

_____

10

Other Wedding Events

By choosing to start a marriage, you and your partner are doing something that is, by its very nature, sacred and intimate. Ironically, those you love best may want to celebrate this very personal thing in an extremely public way. You get engaged and they want to party. Why is this?

I like to think it's because weddings inspire all those good, good feelings that make life worth living. Your loved ones get a taste and want to indulge. Their response is out of your control—and often, it's so heartfelt that you wouldn't want to stop it even if you could. That said, you do have control over an important piece: *how* those people celebrate your love.

Keep this information close as you and your partner consider events outside of your wedding. Identify which bring you joy and which don't. Then—and this part is crucial—communicate those boundaries to your loved ones. If you don't take that challenging but necessary step, you may be invited to parties you don't want to go to.

Your loved ones will plan those parties not because they are rude or bad or inconsiderate but because they're excited! They think this is what you want (or, at least, what every rom-com ever has told them that you want). So if it's not, you need to tell them. That's how you plan events that add to, not detract from, the bliss of the main event: your wedding.

COUPLE 1

Augustin's entire family was traveling internationally to attend his and Gavin's wedding. The expense and time commitment made Augustin feel like he needed to host his family for a post-wedding breakfast even though he knew he'd be exhausted after the wedding. Augustin violated his boundary and hosted an event he barely enjoyed.

COUPLE 2

Kai's parents wanted to plan a big dinner for two nights before Kai and Noah's wedding. While, of course, everyone would have loved to see them, the couple identified that they needed a quiet night in more than they needed another evening out. They communicated this clearly early on. Kai's parents opted to still host the dinner to welcome out-of-town guests, who were told not to expect the couple to make an appearance. Everyone was fine with it.

TOP FIVE ETIQUETTE DOS

1. **Do delegate.** Assign any events that aren't the wedding to someone who isn't you. Give this person the authority to make choices on your behalf so that you're not constantly consulting. Traditional etiquette says you need to bring this person a host gift, but I believe a warm, enthusiastic thank-you at the actual event can go just as far.

2. **Do manage your energy.** Any wedding is a marathon. Follow the same tips you would for running a race: Eat. Sleep. Hydrate.

3. **Do set rules.** Your guests' biggest fear is that they will ruin your wedding. Help them relax by being clear about what you and your partner do and don't expect at certain events. This is particularly useful for any VIPs who are likely going to multiple events. Are they required to buy a gift for every single one?

4. **Do be realistic.** Don't put peer pressure on people you love to do things they can't afford. Find other ways to celebrate if, say, a certain bridesmaid can't afford a long weekend in Vegas. Maybe she can do lunch or a dedicated phone call instead?

5. **Do introduce people.** Introductions are an art that can make a good party great. As the person getting married, you have the most knowledge about who all of these people are in relation to you. Follow this format: "Guest A, let me introduce Guest B, whom I know [insert way you know them]." Bonus points if you then share something beyond you that they have in common to talk about.

TOP FIVE ETIQUETTE DON'TS

1. **Don't be weird about money.** Good manners say it's rude to talk about money, but in my experience, it's ruder to avoid it. Any event host is likely paying for the entire party; consider this as you delegate. Is there a way you can thank this person or let them off the hook for getting you a gift?

2. **Don't get drunk.** It's extremely tempting to cut loose, but you will regret it, particularly if the event is happening right before the wedding. Save your hangover for the honeymoon.

3. **Don't discount premarital counseling.** It can help set you two up for success as you transition your relationship into a marriage. You might also pair this with a conversation about potentially getting a prenup, as relevant to your situation. While some couples may be uncomfortable having these conversations, try not to let lingering stigma hold you back. This isn't as weird as it may sound and has the benefit of serving you long after your wedding day.

4. **Don't forget to say thank you.** Traditional etiquette would require that you write thank-you notes for every single event. While ideal, it isn't always practical and can, unfortunately, have the adverse effect of you not doing anything at all. Avoid this by saying thank you in person. Then follow up with one thank-you note sent *after* the wedding that captures everything that person did for you in relation to the start of your marriage.

5. **Don't fear the power of "no, thank you."** Just because certain wedding events exist doesn't mean you and your partner have to do them or that you have to do them separately. Discuss your options as a couple and then communicate with your VIPs.

ENGAGEMENT PARTY

An engagement party is what it sounds like: a party to celebrate your engagement. Not everyone has one, and if they do, it's often because a member of The Board wants to announce to their community the very big news of a loved one's engagement.

If the latter is your situation, consider using the party as a way to host people you don't want—or, more often, can't afford—to have at your wedding. Be very clear about this with the host and the guests, because default thinking is "If I'm invited to this, I'm invited to the wedding." For example, consider using language on an invite or in a toast such as "While we're not sure how big our wedding will be, we wanted to take this opportunity to celebrate with you."

Here are questions to keep in mind:

▸ Why are we having this event?
▸ What will this event accomplish that our wedding won't?
▸ Who is hosting this event? What are their responsibilities?
▸ Who is paying for this event?
▸ Whom do we want at this event?
▸ When do we want this event to happen?
▸ Where do we want this event to happen?
▸ Have we communicated the above to the host(s)?

CONSIDER THIS

Many wedding events are gendered. This doesn't necessarily have to be a bad thing if, say, you're looking for a way to connect with the women in your life or are long overdue to hang out with your best guy friends. Just be mindful of what you want to accomplish and don't be afraid to buck the norm.

BACHELOR AND BACHELORETTE PARTIES

If the term "bachelor party" or "bachelorette party" makes you break out in a cold sweat, consider what the point of this party is. For some, yes, the point is to wear a hat shaped like a penis and do shots off the nubile body of a consenting stripper.

But it doesn't have to be. This party is meant to gather certain people you care about before you embark on a huge life transition. How you accomplish that goal of togetherness can be as risqué or understated as you want it to be.

As you plan, consider the following:

- Why am I having this event?
- What will this event accomplish that my wedding won't?
- Who is hosting this event? What are their responsibilities?
- Who is paying for this event?
- Whom do I want at this event?
    - The very terms "bachelor" and "bachelorette" are gendered, so if you don't like them, call this something else. Options include "[insert your first name]-a-palooza," "Pre-Wedding Bonanza," and "Friend Party."
- When do I want this event to happen?
    - Please do not do this the night before your wedding unless you are 100 percent confident that you won't drink too much or stay out too late.
- Where do I want this event to happen?
- Have I communicated the above to the host(s)?

THE SHOWER

Historically, a shower helped couples acquire the household items they needed to move in together after they got married.

Unfortunately, this very helpful fundraising function has not caught up with new societal norms. Nobody hosts a shower for a couple who moves in together *before* they get married (though wouldn't that be nice?). Complicating matters further, a shower continues to revolve around an antiquated notion that every wedding has a bride and that the bride is the default manager of the home.

Thankfully, we can toss out these outdated ideas and still retain the power of a shower. We just have to be more intentional in how we direct where that fundraising goes. For example, is it toward a down payment, a kid, or a trip?

It's not impolite to ask for these things, because you're giving people who care about you a chance to contribute toward your marriage. In fact, you're doing them the huge favor of telling them what you want versus leaving them to guess (and, probably, guess wrong).

As you plan, consider the following:

- Why are we having this event?
- What will this event accomplish that our wedding won't?
- Who is hosting this event? What are their responsibilities?
- Who is paying for this event?
- Whom do we want at this event?
  - If you want a gender-specific event, that's okay. If you want to celebrate together in some capacity, that's also okay.
- When do we want this event to happen?
- Where do we want this event to happen?
- Have we communicated the above to the host(s)?

CONSIDER THIS

Use the buying power of any wedding event to make positive change in the world. Does your registry include nonprofits you care about, small businesses you want to support, and/or experiences you want to have together?

REHEARSAL DINNER

Don't be fooled by the word "dinner." This event is any meal you might choose to host after a rehearsal.

Focus on if/how you want to keep hanging out with people. Is it a casual family potluck or a more elaborate affair that includes people who won't be at the rehearsal because they're not in the ceremony? Is this event the day before the wedding or, because of your venue's availability for rehearsals, a few days before?

As you plan, consider the following:

- Why are we having this event?
    - Usually it's to keep the party going, but this event can also serve the dual function of welcoming in people who may be traveling for the wedding and/or introducing VIPs who have never met before.
- What will this event accomplish that our wedding won't?
- Who is hosting this event? What are their responsibilities?
- Who is paying for this event?
    - This is a prime opportunity for a member of The Board to financially contribute. If this is your situation, make sure The Board knows and recognize that it might mean less money for the wedding.
- Whom do we want at this event?
    - Just because someone is in town early does not mean you have to invite them. That said, respect that the event host may want said person to be there.
- When do we want this event to happen?
    - Often, it's going to be right after the rehearsal, but it doesn't have to be. For example, your rehearsal may be in the morning, but you want to get together for dinner, not lunch. Whatever the situation, pick one meal, not two.
- Where do we want this event to happen?
- Have we communicated the above to the host(s)?

CONSIDER THIS

In recent years, weddings have mushroomed from an event that lasts a few hours to lasting a whole day to lasting a whole weekend. Pick the time commitment that serves you and your partner, not others. Short and sweet is just as valid as long and involved.

DAY-AFTER-WEDDING BRUNCH

Couples often plan a day-after-wedding brunch as a last-ditch effort to not be rude to those they may not have had a chance to talk to at the wedding.

Any day-after event can severely eat into a couple's enjoyment of their first day of marriage. As such, proceed with caution. Are you hosting this event because you actually want to see these people again or because you feel compelled to? Could you let someone else take the lead and only attend for 30 or 45 minutes before making a graceful departure?

As you plan, consider the following:

- Why are we having this event?
- What will this event accomplish that our wedding won't?
  - This doesn't have to be formal. The day-after activity might be setting a general time to run into each other at the hotel buffet.
- Who is hosting this event? What are their responsibilities?
- Who is paying for this event?
- Whom do we want at this event?
  - Like the post-rehearsal meal, this event might be an opportunity to let a member of The Board shine, particularly if there are certain guests who matter a lot to them but less to you. Let them host.
- When do we want this event to happen?
  - This is crucial because many weddings go late. Consider what pace you and your partner might want to move at the morning after your wedding and what you may or may not want to do together before seeing other people.
- Where do we want this event to happen?
- Have we communicated the above to the host(s)?

11

Accommodations, Transportation, and More

If you and your partner are like many couples, one of your top wedding planning concerns is ensuring your guests have a good time. This is a worthy goal. Many guests make a huge investment of money and time to attend a wedding. The least we can do is make sure they know how to get from the airport, right? Right.

In nearly all situations, your guests know how to google. More importantly, even if you provide very clear, very easy-to-follow instructions, chances are they'll still default to the internet. It's just habit.

This reality doesn't mean skip this chapter. Rather, use this chapter to revisit those feelings you and your partner want to foster at your wedding. Where someone is staying and how they're getting around can be helpful in inspiring those feelings.

Of course, your guests are adults who can take care of themselves. So as long as they have the most crucial information—when and where to show up on the wedding day—they'll be fine. The people we really need to take care of are you and your partner.

COUPLE 1

Morgan and Dylan forgot to mention how limited parking was at their venue. It was a small mistake that left their guests scrambling to make the ceremony on time. (An easy solution? Include a one- or two-sentence summary on guest-facing correspondence.)

COUPLE 2

Lisa and Sarina wanted an all-out party for their wedding with lots of drinking and hours of dancing. Rather than ask their guests to drive home after, they budgeted for a shuttle between the venue and a centrally located hotel.

TOP FIVE ETIQUETTE DOS

1. **Do give VIPs priority.** These are the people who must be at your wedding in person for it to feel like your wedding. So give them first access to any special arrangements you may be making, like a hotel block or a shuttle.

2. **Do lie about deadlines.** Set any "need information back from guests" deadline a week earlier than you actually need it. This will account for those "I totally forgot!" texts without raising your blood pressure.

3. **Do read your contracts.** In certain situations, you might be on the hook for unfilled rooms or other easy-to-miss details. Carefully review any contract before your sign it and decide if the risk is worth the reward.

4. **Do be clear about what's already covered.** This is most pertinent for your VIPs who likely have more places to be on the wedding day than an average guest does. Are they grabbing a Lyft from one location where they get ready to another location to take photos to a third location to celebrate the wedding? Be clear about who's paying for what so they can plan accordingly.

5. **Do factor in travel time.** You increase the length and cost of your wedding every time you ask guests and vendors to move from one location to another. Keep this in mind as you plan and, where possible, minimize how much people move.

TOP FIVE ETIQUETTE DON'TS

1. **Don't avoid the word "wedding" when making reservations.** For once, the word "wedding" may benefit you in the price department. Mention what the accommodations or transportation is for and just see if you get a little extra something for getting hitched.

2. **Don't overbook.** No matter how well-planned your wedding, you'll have things to do at the last minute. Limit the commitments you make for the two days before your wedding. You don't need to join your guests sightseeing.

3. **Don't stress over welcome bags.** Some couples like to arrange items such as water bottles and sunscreen for their guests to receive upon arrival at a certain destination. It's a nice touch, but if you're going to labor over anything, make it a short and sweet itinerary for the major events they're attending.

4. **Don't worry if you don't arrange anything.** The majority of weddings I've worked haven't arranged any kind of accommodations or transportation for guests. This was totally fine and, in many cases, worked better for the guests who knew their own budgets and tastes best.

5. **Don't forget about you and your partner.** How are you two getting around on the wedding day? Where are you staying at the end of the night? How are you getting there? Do you want to stay together the night before the wedding? (It's okay if you do!)

TRANSPORTATION

Use the first part to brainstorm what, if any, transportation you need to arrange for guests. If you two decide to arrange transportation, use the second part to track your options.

What are the key location(s) of our wedding?

_____

_____

_____

_____

Are any of these locations particularly challenging to get to and from? Consider factors such as distance, traffic, and terrain.

_____

_____

	CONTACT NAME(S) AND PRONOUNS	CONTACT INFORMATION	AVAILABLE FOR OUR WEDDING? (Y/N)
TRANSPORTATION OPTION 1			
TRANSPORTATION OPTION 2			
TRANSPORTATION OPTION 3			

Are there any common qualities about our guests that will make it challenging for them to travel to and from these locations? Consider accessibility, mobility, age, and high number of travelers without cars.

....

....

....

How could we potentially minimize these difficulties?

....

....

Do we have the budget to minimize these difficulties? It's okay to say no.

....

....

TRANSPORTATION SERVICE AND PICK-UP AND DROP-OFF LOCATIONS	PICKUP AND DROP-OFF TIMES	HOW MANY PEOPLE CAN THEY ACCOMMODATE?	FEE	HOW WILL WE COMMUNICATE THESE DETAILS TO THE RELEVANT GUESTS?

ACCOMMODATIONS

Use the first part to brainstorm what, if any, accommodations you need to arrange. If you two decide to arrange accommodations, use the second part to track your options.

What are the key location(s) of our wedding?

....

....

....

....

What are the accommodation options like for these locations? For example, a wedding in the country may have more limited hotel options than a wedding in a city. Other venues offer on-site accommodations such as hotel rooms, cabins, or camping.

....

....

	NAME	CONTACT NAME(S) AND PRONOUNS	CONTACT INFORMATION	AVAILABLE FOR OUR WEDDING? (Y/N)
ACCOMMODATION OPTION 1				
ACCOMMODATION OPTION 2				
ACCOMMODATION OPTION 3				

Are there any day-of wedding events that we need a location for? Consider where you and your partner are each getting ready and if you're getting ready alongside anybody else. Do you need space for this?

Are there any particular guests whom we are concerned about in relation to accommodations? "No" is a completely acceptable response.

How could we potentially minimize these difficulties?

Do we have the budget to minimize these difficulties? It's okay to say no.

WHICH GUESTS IS THIS OPTION FOR?	ARE THERE ANY DEADLINES WE NEED TO KEEP IN MIND?	RATE (SPECIFY IF THE GUESTS ARE PAYING FOR ANY PORTION OF THE SERVICE)	WHEN IS CHECK-IN? WHEN IS CHECKOUT?	HOW WILL WE COMMUNICATE THESE DETAILS TO THE RELEVANT GUESTS?

ACTIVITIES FOR OUT-OF-TOWN GUESTS

If you want to provide additional ideas, use these questions to brainstorm.

▶ **Are there holes in the schedule that we want to fill?**

▶ **Why do we want to fill them?**

▶ **Are there certain details about the place where we're hosting our wedding that we want to share with our guests?**

▶ **Is anybody arriving early for our wedding whom we want to accommodate?** Often these are relatives or guests who are traveling internationally.

▶ **What kind of activities might this person or people like?** Consider interests, duration, and travel time to and from.

▶ **Are any of these activities things we want to participate in ourselves leading up to our wedding?** "No" is a completely acceptable response.

▶ **If any of these activities cost money, who's paying for what?**

▶ **How will we communicate these details to the relevant guests?**

12

Wedding Day

You've made it! After hours of work and thousands of dollars, your wedding day is nearly here. If you're like 99.9 percent of couples, that thought excites you as much as it terrifies you.

Usually, this pre-wedding stress manifests in one of two ways: A couple either grabs on or shuts down.

The first reaction looks like a bunch of increasingly frantic messages sent in the wee hours of the morning. If this person identifies as a woman, you might hear her called a "bridezilla." (In my opinion, that's just another bad word we call women.)

The second reaction looks like a lot of shrugging. This person takes an increasingly long time to reply to messages, and if they do reply, they default to "I don't care" or "Whatever you want." This reaction is the more common of the two because nobody wants to be equated with a giant radioactive sea monster.

The good news? Neither reaction has to be your fate. If we approach your big day with intention, you can actually go to your wedding and enjoy it! Here's how to do that.

COUPLE 1

On his wedding day, Connor had a nasty habit of saying, "Just tell me where to be." While he meant it in jest, the phrase made it seem like he didn't actually care what happened on his wedding day. Connor should have challenged himself to play a more active role in the event.

COUPLE 2

Luis and Tanya made a vow to stay by each other's side throughout the wedding reception. Though they weren't always able to stick to it, the goal served as a guiding star amid the wedding hubbub. Anytime they found themselves separate, they worked to get back to each other so they could experience the day together.

TOP FIVE ETIQUETTE DOS

1. **Do eat.** Regular meals and hydration are key to enjoying your wedding day. Plan to eat at least a little before you put on your fancy clothes or finish any hair and makeup.

2. **Do what you like.** Just because this is your wedding day doesn't mean you can't do what you like. Not a morning person? Don't schedule hair and makeup to start at dawn. Always feel better after yoga? Book a session.

3. **Do take time for just the two of you.** A natural time for this is right after the ceremony or later in the day during what's often known as the "golden hour" (a great time to take pictures). Build in time to step away, if only for 15 or 20 minutes, so you and your partner can take in this big thing that just happened to you both.

4. **Do say thank you to your vendors.** This doesn't have to be a big production. A simple "thank you for your work" or, as appropriate, a quick hug can mean a world of difference to the team that helped you pull off this whole thing.

5. **Do prioritize.** While you won't have time to say hi to everyone, you know who's extra special, whether they're a beloved older relative or a friend from the other side of the world. Make a point to say hi to them.

TOP FIVE ETIQUETTE DON'TS

1. **Don't play timekeeper.** Assign someone else this role so that, as much as possible, you can disconnect from your phone and be present with your loved ones. This same person can prep the infamous "day-of-wedding emergency kit." (My two cents: You'll already have a lot of this stuff anyway, but, sure, put it in a nice bag if you want!)

2. **Don't expect to say hi to everyone.** It's nice to make an effort, but if you find yourself getting caught up gazing into your new spouse's eyes, prioritize that instead. To cover your bases, consider saying a few short words of welcome during the wedding, if public speaking doesn't terrify you.

3. **Don't forget that this is a big day for other people, too.** Often, this means The Board, who in some cases may have been thinking about this day for your whole life. Give them space to feel their feelings. If you feel moved to do so, acknowledge all they've done to help you get to this point.

4. **Don't rush.** No matter how you build it, your wedding day will feel fast. Challenge yourself to take a deep breath and look around. What do you see, smell, taste, hear, and feel? Take a photo with your mind.

5. **Don't feel bad if you don't have sex.** You will be tired. You might be drunk. It's okay if you skip the infamous wedding night. You'll have plenty of time to catch up later (including the next morning).

THE DAY IS HERE

As a professional wedding planner, I thought I knew what my wedding day would feel like. I had, after all, been to more weddings than most people go to in a lifetime. And yet, despite this extensive experience, my wedding day felt unlike anything I ever have and, potentially, ever will feel again.

The same will be true for you. You can listen to the music, wear the clothes, and taste the food and, still, your wedding day will exceed all expectations. That's exactly how it should be because a wedding day isn't just a wedding day. It's the start of something new. It's the birth of your marriage.

As you think about what to expect and how to plan for your wedding, give yourself a lot of grace. The ritual and beauty of a wedding ceremony may stir feelings in you that you never expected. A particular toast might inspire an emotion you couldn't anticipate. I can guarantee you that the most special moment will be the one you didn't plan for.

Let that magic flow. You've done the hard work. Now, let go and enjoy.

THE REHEARSAL

Please don't skip the rehearsal. It may feel unnecessary or seem like more trouble than it's worth, but trust me: It's not. A rehearsal serves a very particular function: It gets the wiggles out and helps people visualize the main event.

As you plan, consider the following:

- **Who's in charge?** Bestow managerial duties on a VIP or vendor. Have them huddle everyone up, introduce themselves, and then cruise direct.
- **Where are we having this?** Ideally, the same spot as the ceremony, but if that's not possible, still have a rehearsal. A living room or backyard works just as well.
- **Who's walking when?** Decide and communicate this *before* the rehearsal.
- **In what order do we want people to go down the aisle?** Here's one completely optional template:
  - Officiant(s)
  - Partner 1, alone or alongside a VIP
  - Any older and respected VIPs, such as a grandparent or a parent, sometimes accompanied by another VIP
  - First pair, second pair, etc.

  Note: *Some couples prefer to have one party enter from the side and the other party go down the aisle single file.*
  - Ring bearer(s)

Note: *If you prefer not to have a ring bearer but have wedding rings to exchange, just pick a VIP or the officiant to hold on to the rings.*

- ► Flower person or people
- ► Partner 2, alone or alongside a VIP
- ► **Which song(s), if any, do we want play?** It's helpful to tell the people who are going down the aisle what to listen for so they know when to go. You don't actually have to play the music during the rehearsal.
- ► **What's happening during our ceremony?** Hit the highlights and finalize cues for anybody who's doing something during the ceremony such as a reading, a song, handing over the rings, etc.
- ► **Are there any seats we need to save?** On the wedding day, I often tape a "reserved" sign with the person's name on it to their chair.
- ► **Is anybody not here whom we need to update?** If a VIP couldn't make the rehearsal, brief them afterward as needed.
- ► **Where's our license?** Know where your license is and how it's getting to the ceremony.

CONSIDER THIS

Many ceremonies include—to use an inelegant term—props. Think: rings, vows, readings, candles, sand, rope, brooms, and glasses. Assign someone to make sure these things get where they need to go on the wedding day.

WEDDING DAY PACKING LIST

- ☐ License
- ☐ Ring(s)
- ☐ Vow(s)
- ☐ Tip(s)
- ☐ Any necessary medication

- ☐ What you're wearing to your wedding, including shoes, accessories, and/or undergarments
- ☐ Any cards or gifts you may have for your partner, VIPs, and/ or vendors

- [ ] Any changes of clothes for during the day and/or the end of the night
- [ ] Snacks and a water bottle (alternatively, arrange for food and drink to be available wherever you're getting ready)
- [ ] Toiletries for during the day and/or the end of the night
- [ ] If you're leaving on a trip immediately after your wedding, anything you may need for that trip, including passports, cash, spare keys for house-sitters, etc.
- [ ] Decorations—many venues won't let you leave things overnight, so you'll likely need to assign someone to get these items from Point A (you) to Point B (the venue(s) before the wedding)

CONSIDER THIS

The receiving line may seem outdated, but it's actually an efficient way to do a very cool thing: Say hi to everyone at your wedding. Plus, as an extra-special thank-you, invite The Board to join you in line.

OUR CEREMONY

Do not be fooled: The ceremony, not the reception, is the beating heart of your wedding. The reception is important and fun; it may even be where you feel most like yourself. But the ceremony is where the magic happens. As you plan your ceremony, consider the following.

- **How do we want to feel during our ceremony?** Refer to the "Our Ideal Ceremony Worksheet" in chapter 4 (page 42).
- **What activities are happening during our ceremony?** Here's a loose order of operations:
  - The processional (who walks down the aisle)
  - Opening and welcome from the officiant(s)
  - Any readings, songs, prayers, etc.
  - Vows and/or "I dos"
  - Ring exchange

- ▸ Pronouncement (when the officiant(s) say you're married now)
- ▸ The kiss
- ▸ The recessional (you walk back up the aisle)
- ▸ **What items do we need for each activity? Who will be in charge of each item?** (Who's holding the vows? The rings? Any other ceremony props? Tissues?)
- ▸ **When are we signing the license?** Usually, this is done right after the ceremony, away from guests.

CONSIDER THIS

Is a beloved animal going to be part of your wedding? Assign a pet handler to make sure your fur baby gets what they need, too. This can be a guest, a friend, or, budget permitting, a professional (yes, wedding pet-sitting services exist!).

OUR VOWS

The vows are the words you and your partner say to each other to signify the start of your marriage. Some couples love the challenge. Others are terrified of saying the wrong thing.

Talk to your partner about how you two want to feel during your ceremony and decide what role vows play in creating that feeling. There are lots of ways this can take place, from the call-and-repeat structure familiar from more religious ceremonies to pre-writing a list of promises that you recite to each other to both secretly crafting short paragraphs specific to your partner. When in doubt, consult templates online or sign up for a vow writing workshop (a real thing you can do together!).

As you think about vows, reflect on these prompts.

- ▸ In our vows, do we want to highlight any of our answers from the "Shared Values Worksheet" in chapter 1 (page 4)?
- ▸ *If you're writing your vows together:*
  - ▸ What are the top three reasons we're excited to marry each other?
  - ▸ How do we want to feel during our ceremony? Are there certain memories, quotes, and/or visuals that would help?

- *If you're writing your own vows in secret:*
  - What are the top three reasons I'm excited to marry this particular person?
  - How do I want my partner to feel during our ceremony? Are there certain memories, quotes, and/or visuals that would help?

CONSIDER THIS

You can seat your particular VIPs on the side opposite from where you'll be positioned at the front of the ceremony space. This bucks tradition but allows your most valued loved ones to see your face during the ceremony.

OUR RECEPTION

The reception is the first party that you and your partner will attend as a married couple. Make the most of it! As you plan, consider the following.

What activities are happening during our reception? Here's a loose order of operations:
- Couple introduction (if this strikes fear into your hearts, skip it; if it doesn't, keep it in because guests appreciate knowing when you two arrive)
- Main meal
- Toast(s)
- First bite (best to do before any dancing so you can keep the spotlight moving in one fluid motion)
- First dance(s)
- Dance floor opens
- Bouquet and/or garter toss
- Any additional wedding "traditions" or reception programming
- Sunset or "golden hour" photos (may be earlier depending on what time of year you're having your wedding)
- Last call (most important for your guests)
- Couple leaves

- ▶ Guests leave (usually throughout the reception and/or right after you two depart)
- ▶ Venue rental ends (allocate at least an hour starting from when guests leave)

CONSIDER THIS

You don't have to stay for the whole reception. In fact, you might be done in by hour two. If that sounds like you and your partner, own it, but don't disappear. Give your guests a chance to say goodbye, perhaps with a quick announcement by the MC.

THE WEDDING DAY TIMELINE

The template below is for a wedding day timeline. It includes a variety of options, so pick and choose what applies to you and your partner.

- ◆ [date] .... — Apply for marriage license

- ◆ [date] .... — Rehearsal at [location] ....

The Wedding Day

- ◆ [time] .... — Hair and/or makeup appointments for

  [whom] .... at [location] ....

- ◆ [time] .... — Venue rental begins at

  [location] ....

- ◆ [time] .... — Florist and/or flowers arrive at

  [location] ....

- ◆ [time] .... — Photographer(s) begin at

  [location] ....

- ♦ *Dedicate 30 minutes for each option that follows. A photographer will likely start an hour before the first round of photos to capture what are known as "getting-ready" photos.*

- ♦ [time] .... — *If before the ceremony:*

  First look begins at [location] ....

- ♦ [time] .... — *If after the ceremony:*

  Couple photos begin at [location] ....

- ♦ [time] .... — Wedding party photos begin at

  [location] ....

  - ♦ *In this instance, "party" refers to the VIPs who may be accompanying a certain partner during the ceremony.*

- ♦ [time] .... — Family photos begin at

  [location] ....

- ♦ [time] .... — Videographer(s) begin at

  [location] ....

- ♦ [time] .... — Ceremony music arrives at

  [location] ....

- ♦ [time] .... — Reception music arrives at

  [location] ....

- ♦ [time] .... — Caterer(s) arrive at

  [location] ....

- ♦ [time] .... — Dessert arrives at

  [location] ....

- ♦ [time] .... — Officiant(s) arrive at

  [location] ....

- ◆ [time] _____ — Partner 1 and their party get
  ready at [location] _____

- ◆ [time] _____ — Partner 2 and their party get
  ready at [location] _____

- ◆ [time] _____ — Partner 1 and their party take
  [mode of transportation] _____ to arrive at
  [location] _____

- ◆ [time] _____ — Partner 2 and their party take
  [mode of transportation] _____ to arrive at
  [location] _____

  - ◆ *To decide your ceremony time, first figure out when you want to take photos (before or after). Then, count back from there.*

- ◆ [time] _____ — Ceremony begins at
  [location] _____

- ◆ [time] _____ — Couple signs license at
  [location] _____ with
  [name of witness 1] _____ and
  [name of witness 2] _____ and officiant

- ◆ [time] _____ — Reception begins at
  [location] _____

- ◆ [time] _____ — Couple introduced as
  [couple's preferred name(s) for an introduction] _____

- *Photos need light, so it makes a difference when the sun goes down.*

- [time] .... — Sunset

- [time] .... — Main meal begins

- [time] .... — Toast(s)

- [time] .... — First bite

- [time] .... — First dance(s)

- [time] .... — Dance floor opens

- [time] .... — Bouquet and/or garter toss

- [time] .... — Any additional wedding traditions

- [time] .... — Last call

- [time] .... — Couple leaves via

  [mode of transportation] .... to

  [location] ....

- [time] .... — Guests leave

- [time] .... — Venue rental ends

  - *Alcohol*: goes with [name of person] ....

  - *Decorations*: go with [name of person] ....

  - *Gifts*: go with [name of person] ....

  - *Leftover food*: goes with [name of person] ....

WHOM SHOULD WE TIP?

- **Bar** (only if gratuity isn't already included): $15 to $20 per person
- **Hair and/or makeup** (highly recommended): 15 to 20 percent
- **Florist** (nice if they've been awesome but not required): 10 to 15 percent
- **Food** (only if gratuity isn't already included): 15 to 20 percent, or $30 to $50 per chef and $15 to $20 per server
- **Music** (highly recommended because they've lugged so much equipment around)
  - band — $25 to $50 per band member
  - DJ — 10 to 15 percent
- **Officiant** (nice if they've been awesome but not required): 10 to 15 percent or $100 donation to the institution where they're ordained
- **Photographer and/or videographer** (nice if they've been awesome but not required): $50 to $200
- **Rental delivery** (highly recommended if setup and/or teardown is involved): $10 to $15 per person
- **Transportation** (only do if gratuity isn't already included): 15 percent
- **Venue staff** (nice if they've been awesome but not required): $15 to $20 per person
- **Wedding coordinator** (nice if they've been awesome but not required): 10 to 15 percent

13

Post-Wedding Happenings

You did it! You had a wedding, and now you're married. Please take this opportunity to grab your spouse and give them a big kiss.

All done? Welcome back. In this chapter, we will discuss tying up those final loose ends so that you and your love can officially close the book on wedding planning (get it?) and move on with your lives.

Before we go, I want to say thank you. Thank you for letting me accompany you on this journey. It's very easy to minimize the deeply personal experience of planning a wedding, but I believe a wedding—and the planning it entails—is one of society's most joyful rituals. Not everybody does it. Not everybody wants or needs to do it. But those who do are different people by the end of it, and that, my friend, is worth a moment of reflection.

How are you different from the person you were when you got engaged? How was planning your wedding better and worse than you anticipated? What did you learn about your partner? What did your partner learn about you? These are valuable questions to ask as you embark on what is, without a doubt, the much cooler adventure: your marriage.

I wish you all the luck in the world. And, again, thank you for having me come along. It's been an honor.

COUPLE 1

Chris's stepmom insisted on hosting a post-wedding brunch to maximize time with out-of-town relatives. Rather than tell his mom that he didn't want to go or could only attend for a short time, Chris blew off the brunch entirely. His mom (and his relatives) were disappointed and confused.

COUPLE 2

Before leaving on their honeymoon, Kevin and Jameela made sure all their vendors were paid in full. They recognized that these final payments were the money their vendors used to feed their families and pay any employees.

TOP FIVE ETIQUETTE DOS

1. **Do write reviews.** You don't have to do it right away. In fact, you may be best served by carving out an hour a month after your wedding to write online reviews for each of your vendors. It's a small gesture that makes a huge difference.

2. **Do send thank-you cards.** As previously discussed in this book, it's ideal if you send a thank-you card after every wedding-related happening, but that's often not possible. Instead, opt for one round after your wedding. Consider this simple format: one sentence to say thank you, one sentence to highlight a detail specific to the receiver(s), and one sentence to sign off.

3. **Do remember rentals.** If you followed advice shared earlier in this book, you've already assigned certain people to return certain items, as applicable. If not, do this now. If it's a last-minute request, consider a $5 gift card or short thank-you note for the person you asked.

4. **Do mail your license.** In many parts of the United States, there's a specific window of time after the ceremony when you can return your license. Sometimes it's quite short, so play it safe and drop your license in the mail before you peace out.

5. **Do tell people what you want to be called.** If you and/or your partner are changing any part of your name(s), make an announcement. (A bcc'd email works great.) You'll need to request what's known as a "certified copy" of your license to file the name-change paperwork. Ask for this when you mail your license (page 186) to save you a step after the wedding.

TOP FIVE ETIQUETTE DON'TS

1. **Don't undervalue time off.** However your wedding shook out, you're going to be tired. If at all possible, please plan to take at least one day off before you return to your regular programming. You don't have to go anywhere; a quiet day at home can work wonders.

2. **Don't overcommit.** Post-wedding meals? Rides to the airport? Final good-byes? Only sign up for these as makes sense for your and your partner's energy. You may feel like you owe your guests more face time, but they got what they came for: to see you two get married.

3. **Don't forget who has what.** It's rude to leave all of your wedding stuff in your best friend's garage for weeks on end unless that's what you and your friend previously discussed. Make a clear and timely pickup plan.

4. **Don't pressure your vendors.** Photos and video take time, which is why it'll likely be at least six weeks before you see any digital evidence of your wedding. When you do and if you have feedback, be specific and keep in mind how many free rounds of edits your contract does (or does not) allow.

5. **Don't expect to feel the same.** Many couples say that nothing changed after they got married. If that's true for you two, great! Live that life. If it's not true, that's also okay. Give yourselves time and space to appreciate this big thing you just did together.

HONEYMOON

Couples often tell me that they had more fun planning their honeymoon than they did planning their wedding. Given the nature of this book, I hope that isn't the case for you two. Still, the honeymoon can be a fun time to indulge in a shared dream. It's also a crucial time to transition into this new thing called marriage.

No matter how long you two have been a couple or whether or not you lived together before getting married, a very big change just happened. Use the time right after your wedding to explore your new role in each other's life. What does this very public, very legal transition mean to your relationship? What are you two calling each other now? How is each of you feeling?

Plan a honeymoon that aligns with those questions. Go as far away or stay as close to home as makes sense for your budget, work, and energy. A one-day stay-cation can be just as meaningful as two weeks in Fiji. The point is to do it together, as a married couple. See the honeymoon as a time to reacquaint yourselves, take a breath, and return refreshed to begin the real work of maintaining a marriage.

HONEYMOON INSPIRATION WORKSHEET

What was our favorite trip together ever?

....

....

....

....

Are there elements of that trip that we'd like to mirror in our honeymoon?

....

....

....

....

If we could do anything in the world after our wedding, what would it be and why?

....

....

....

....

What are three adjectives we would use to describe this ideal honeymoon?

....

How do we want our honeymoon to make us feel?

....

....

....

What is our ideal budget for this honeymoon? Consider all elements, including renewing passports, buying new luggage, excursions, meals, etc. Remember that you could potentially ask for some of these elements to be paid for through your registry.

....

....

....

When is our ideal time to take this honeymoon?

....

....

....

BOOKING A HONEYMOON CHECKLIST

Before Our Wedding

- ☐ Decide on location(s).
- ☐ Research any vaccinations and/or documentation we need to travel.
- ☐ Book travel.
- ☐ Book accommodations.
- ☐ Consider adding excursions, meals, and other trip-related expenses to our registry. As applicable, book these separately.
- ☐ Arrange any child, pet, and/or plant care for while we're away, as applicable.
- ☐ Confirm a ride to the airport and/or transportation home, as applicable.
- ☐ Decide what items, including leftover food, we'll have after our wedding that we don't want to take on the honeymoon. Whom are we giving these items to and when?
- ☐ Pack. (Ideally, this will be in bags separate from any bags you pack for the wedding itself.)
- ☐ Double-check if we owe any vendors money on or after our wedding.

After Our Wedding but Before We Leave

- ☐ Mail our marriage license.
- ☐ Pay any vendors.
- ☐ Hand off any rentals and/or time-sensitive items to be returned during our absence.

THANK-YOU CARDS

Thank-you cards make people groan because, omg, we still have work to do? Thankfully, this last hurdle isn't as hard as it seems.

Divide and conquer as a couple, assigning half of the thank-yous to your partner and half to yourself. Keep the message short and sweet. Three sentences are plenty, particularly if one of those sentences includes a detail that shows you actually know what this person did on your behalf.

If you're really strapped for time, consider the one-and-done thank-you. This is a pre-made thank-you card or postcard that may feature a photo from your wedding and doesn't have any customized note or other message. This option isn't as personal or heartfelt as a handwritten note, but it at least acknowledges the effort of the person you're writing to. Perhaps add a line or two specific to the person if they're a member of The Board or other VIP.

As for your vendors? A thank-you note is lovely to receive but a tip and/or online review means more. So if you're strapped for time, money, and brainpower, don't worry about a thank-you card for a vendor.

When do you do all this stuff? Ideally, within the first three months of your marriage; however, if more time has passed, still do this. Saying thank you is always in style.

Finally, consider your thank-you cards as a way to support a small business. Research local print shops. Perhaps consider buying a smaller batch of letterpress thank-yous for your VIPs and going with a cheaper option for other guests. Don't sweat having the thank-you notes match the aesthetic of your wedding or whether or not they include a photo from the day, The goal is to get these out so you can move on with your life.

CONSIDER THIS

Wedding photos make excellent gifts. For the first major holiday following your wedding, consider printing off and, budget and time permitting, framing specific photos to give to your VIPs. It's a lovely and fairly affordable way to relive an important day.

VENDOR REVIEW CHECKLIST

☐ **Look at your list of vendors.**

Note who did a good job or a bad job.

☐ **Start with the vendors who did a good job.**

Write a three- to five-sentence review that explains who you are in relation to this person, one thing you liked about them, and if you recommend their work to others. Google their business, see where they have online reviews, and copy and paste what you wrote to each platform. No need to tell your vendor you wrote reviews; they'll get an automated email.

☐ **Move on to the vendors who did a bad job.**

Rather than bash them online, send a thoughtful email explaining what they could have done better. If they violated your contract or, heaven forbid, caused harm at your wedding, ask for what you want as retribution, such as a credit toward a future service or a refund. Use the email to ask for a call if the conversation is particularly sensitive.

CONSIDER THIS

Do you two want a wedding album? Many photographers will make these on your behalf for an additional fee. There are also tons of online options and DIY alternatives. Albums can be quite expensive. There's no obligation to create one right away or at all.

POST-WEDDING CHECKLIST

☐ **Have we requested and/or received the certified copies of our marriage license?**

Use these to change any name(s), as applicable. Save at least one copy in a secure location.

- ☐ Have we updated any online presence and/or employers about any changes resulting from our marriage?

    Think: name, address, email address, relationship status, etc.

- ☐ Have we updated any legal paperwork to make our spouse our next of kin or beneficiary?

    Think: health insurance, retirement accounts, leases, deeds, wills, medical documentation, etc.

- ☐ Have we decided how we want to file our tax return next year?
- ☐ Have we decided what, if anything, we want to do with the decorative version of our marriage license?

    This is the fancy one you signed but didn't need to mail. Consider framing and hanging it in your home or putting it in a wedding album.

APPENDIX:
IMPORTANT NAMES AND CONTACT INFORMATION

This template is for a vendor directory. It includes a variety of options, so pick and choose what applies to you and your partner.

ALCOHOL (INCLUDE WHO'S SUPPLYING IT AND WHO'S POURING IT)

- Name(s) and Pronouns: _____

- Phone: _____

- Email: _____

- Name(s) and Pronouns: _____

- Phone: _____

- Email: _____

CATERER(S) (ALL MEALS)

- Name(s) and Pronouns: _____

- Phone: _____

- Email: _____

CEREMONY AND/OR RECEPTION MUSIC

- ▶ Name(s) and Pronouns: _____

- ▶ Phone: _____

- ▶ Email: _____

CLOTHING (INCLUDING ANY ALTERATIONS OR TAILORING)

- ▶ Name(s) and Pronouns: _____

- ▶ Phone: _____

- ▶ Email: _____

- ▶ Name(s) and Pronouns: _____

- ▶ Phone: _____

- ▶ Email: _____

DESSERT

- ▶ Name(s) and Pronouns: _____

- ▶ Phone: _____

- ▶ Email: _____

FLORIST AND/OR FLOWERS

▶ Name(s) and Pronouns: _____

▶ Phone: _____

▶ Email: _____

HAIR AND/OR MAKEUP

▶ Name(s) and Pronouns: _____

▶ Phone: _____

▶ Email: _____

OFFICIANT(S)

▶ Name(s) and Pronouns: _____

▶ Phone: _____

▶ Email: _____

PHOTOGRAPHER(S)

▶ Name(s) and Pronouns: _____

▶ Phone: _____

▶ Email: _____

REHEARSAL MEAL AND/OR LOCATION

- ▶ Name(s) and Pronouns: _____
- ▶ Phone: _____
- ▶ Email: _____

RENTALS

- ▶ Name(s) and Pronouns: _____
- ▶ Phone: _____
- ▶ Email: _____

TRANSPORTATION

- ▶ Name(s) and Pronouns: _____
- ▶ Phone: _____
- ▶ Email: _____

VENUE(S) (CEREMONY AND RECEPTION)

- ▶ Name(s) and Pronouns: _____
- ▶ Phone: _____
- ▶ Email: _____

- ▶ Name(s) and Pronouns: ....
- ▶ Phone: ....
- ▶ Email: ....

VIDEOGRAPHER(S)

- ▶ Name(s) and Pronouns: ....
- ▶ Phone: ....
- ▶ Email: ....

WEDDING COORDINATOR(S) OR PLANNER(S)

- ▶ Name(s) and Pronouns: ....
- ▶ Phone: ....
- ▶ Email: ....

ADDITIONAL RESOURCES

BOOKS

- *Elope Your Life: A Guide to Living Authentically and Unapologetically, Starting With "I Do"* by Sam Starns
- *Equally Wed: The Ultimate Guide to Planning Your LGBTQ+ Wedding* by Kirsten Palladino
- *Marriage, a History* by Stephanie Coontz
- *Offbeat Bride: Creative Alternatives for Independent Brides* by Ariel Meadow Stallings
- *One Perfect Day: The Selling of the American Wedding* by Rebecca Mead
- *A Practical Wedding: Creative Ideas for Planning a Beautiful, Affordable, and Meaningful Celebration* by Meg Keene
- *The Wedding Roller Coaster: Keeping Your Relationships Intact Through the Ups and Downs* by Leah Weinberg
- Literally any other book that's not about weddings, because you do have other interests even if the wedding industrial complex makes it easy to feel like you shouldn't.

NOT-GROSS WEDDING ORGANIZATIONS

- Altared, *Altaredpdx.com* (Disclosure: I'm a co-founder.)
- Green Wedding Guild, *GreenWeddingGuild.com*
- Less Stuff, More Meaning, *LessStuffMoreMeaning.org*
- National Gay Wedding Association, *NationalGayWeddingAssociation.org*
- Unity Through Community, *Terricainc.com/unity-through-community*
- Wedding & Event Vendor Alliance, *Wevavt.org*

PODCASTS

- *Bridechilla*
- *Put a Ring On It*
- *The Teardown* (I'm the host.)

UNIQUE SERVICES FOR COUPLES

- Dash of Pride, *DashofPride.com*
- The Experiential Wedding, *TheExperientialWedding.com*
- Less Stuff, More Meaning Wedding Footprint Calculator, *LessStuffMoreMeaning.org/weddingfootprintcalculator*
- Lori Mason Design Studio, *LoriMasonDesign.com* (Make a wedding quilt!)
- Your Love Profiles, *YourLoveProfiles.com* (Look for the "Premarital Prep Program.")

UNIQUE SERVICES FOR WEDDING VENDORS

- Crystal Whiteaker, *CrystalLily.co*
- Erin Perkins, *MabelyQ.com*
- Jen Siomacco, *VVitchDigital.com*
- Jordan Maney, *JordanManey.com*
- Taylor de la Fuente, *ltEditorial.com*
- Terrica, *TerricaInc.com*

WEDDING PLANNING WEBSITES AND VENDOR DIRECTORIES

- The B Collective, *TheBCollective.co*
- Black Gay Weddings, *BlackGayWeddings.com*
- Catalyst Wed Co., *CatalystWedCo.com*
- Equally Wed, *EquallyWed.com*
- Mandala Weddings, *MandalaWeddings.com*
- MunaLuchi Bride, *MunaLuchiBridal.com*
- Offbeat Bride, *OffbeatBride.com*
- A Practical Wedding, *APracticalWedding.com*
- Vendors of Color, *VendorsofColor.com*

REFERENCES

Casserly, Meghan. "Women, Work & Weddings." *Forbes.* July 22, 2010. Forbes
.com/2010/07/22/wedding-planning-the-knot-wedding-channel-websites-
forbes-woman-time-working-brides-survey.html?sh=5642fc2a3af8.

Horowitz, Juliana Menasce, Nikki Graf, and Gretchen Livingston. "Marriage and
Cohabitation in the U.S." Pew Research Center. November 6, 2019. Pew
Research.org/social-trends/2019/11/06/marriage-and-cohabitation-in-the-u-s.

Lee, Esther. "This Was the Average Cost of a Wedding in 2020." The Knot. Last
modified February 11, 2021. TheKnot.com/content/average-wedding-cost.

Perschbacher, Emily. "How to Plan an Eco-Friendly Wedding." *Chicago
Tribune.* May 30, 2017. ChicagoTribune.com/lifestyles/sc-green-wedding
-family-0530-20170526-story.html.

PRNewswire. "Couples Spend an Average of $33,931 on Weddings, Creating
Completely Personalized Celebrations With Emphasis on Reclaiming and
Redefining Tradition, According to The Knot 2018 Real Weddings Study."
February 14, 2019. PRNewswire.com/news-releases/couples-spend-an
-average-of-33-931-on-weddings-creating-completely-personalized
-celebrations-with-emphasis-on-reclaiming-and-redefining-tradition
-according-to-the-knot-2018-real-weddings-study-300795628.html.

Segran, Elizabeth. "Zola's Plan to Take On the $72 Billion Wedding Industry." *Fast
Company.* August 6, 2018. FastCompany.com/90212949/zolas-plan-to-take
-on-the-72-billion-wedding-industry.

"Wedding Footprint Calculator." Less Stuff, More Meaning. Accessed May 10,
2021. LessStuffMoreMeaning.org/weddingfootprintcalculator.

INDEX

ACKNOWLEDGMENTS

This part always seems to end with the most important person, but this book is all about reexamining old traditions, so I'd like to start with my husband. Jay, I love you. You are why I do this job. Thank you for your love and our family.

Mom, Dad, Izzy, Nick, Jacque, Mike, Jill, Matthew, Pearl, Julie, Syd, Julie, Kerry, Jay, Stephanie, Marshall, Isabelle, Grandma, and Grandpa, thank you for always showing me what love looks like.

Ross and Nicole, your generosity and expertise are why I felt like I could even do this.

John and the team at Callisto, thank you for giving me a chance.

My couples and vendor friends, you inspire me to keep fighting.

ABOUT THE AUTHOR

 **Elisabeth "Beth" Kramer** (she/her) is a wedding planner in Portland, Oregon, who is fighting the wedding industrial complex. She does this through her work with couples (she actively coordinates weddings) and through her work with vendors—she is the host of the podcast *The Teardown* and co-founder of Altared, an international event for wedding vendors who want to change the wedding industry. Learn more about her work at ElisabethKramer.com.

CPSIA information can be obtained
at www.ICGtesting.com
Printed in the USA
JSHW051518030921
18386JS00002B/2

9 781638 074106